The Deeper Meaning of Liff

Douglas Adams is the creator of *Dirk Gently*, *Last Chance to See* and all five volumes of *The Hitchhiker's Guide to the Galaxy* trilogy. He has a magnificent pulverbatch.

John Lloyd is the producer behind *Not the Nine O'Clock News*, *Spitting Image*, *Blackadder* and a number of affcots.

The Deeper Meaning of Liff

Douglas Adams
and John Lloyd

Illuminated by
Bert Kitchen

HARMONY BOOKS
New York

Copyright © 1990 by Serious Productions Ltd. and John Lloyd
Illustrations copyright © 1990 by Bert Kitchen
Published by Harmony Books, a division of Crown Publishers, Inc., 201 East 50th
Street, New York, New York 10022. Member of the Crown Publishing Group.
Originally published in slightly different form in Great Britain by
Pan Books Limited and Faber & Faber Limited in 1990.
Random House, Inc. New York, Toronto, London, Sydney, Auckland
HARMONY and colophon are trademarks of Crown Publishers, Inc.
Manufactured in U.S.A.
Design by Mercedes Everett
Maps by Jason Küffer
Library of Congress Cataloging-in-Publication Data
Adams, Douglas
The deeper meaning of liff : a dictionary of things there aren't
any words for yet—but there ought to be / Douglas Adams & John
Lloyd ; illuminated by Bert Kitchen.
p. cm.
Rev. ed. of: The meaning of liff. c1984.
Includes index.
I. English language—Terms and phrases—Humor. 2. English
language—Humor. 3. English wit and humor. I. Lloyd, John, 1951-
. II. Adams, Douglas, 1952- Meaning of liff. III. Title.
PN6231.W64A33 1993
428.1'0207—dc20 93-25255
CIP
ISBN 0-517-58597-9
10 9 8 7 6 5 4 3 2 1
First American Edition

Contents

Prefaces

Preface to *The Meaning of Liff*, 1983

In Life * there are many hundreds of common experiences, feelings, situations and even objects which we will all know and recognize, but for which no word exists. On the other hand, the world is littered with thousands of spare words which spend their time doing nothing but loafing about on signposts pointing at places. Our job, as we see it, is to get these words down off the signposts and into the mouths of babes and sucklings and so on, where they can start earning their keep in everyday conversation and make a more positive contribution to society.

Douglas Adams, John Lloyd, Malibu, 1982

Preface to the 1984 Reprint

What we said in the first preface pretty much stands, I think.

Douglas Adams, New York, 1983

Preface to the Second 1984 Reprint

Can't think of anything much to add to the previous preface. It's nice, here, though.

Douglas Adams, Seychelles, 1984

Is it?

John Lloyd, Birmingham, 1984

* And, indeed, in Liff.

Preface to the 1986 Reprint

There was a point I was going to make in this preface but it's one of those things that you just can't remember when you actually sit down to write it.

Douglas Adams, Madagascar, 1985

Preface to the 1987 Reprint

No. It came back to me briefly when I was in Brazil, but I didn't have a pen with me.

Douglas Adams, Hong Kong, 1986

Preface to the 1988 Reprint

Did you get the preface I faxed you from New Zealand?

Douglas Adams, Zaire, 1988

Preface to the 1989 Reprint

No.

John Lloyd, Lambeth, 1989

Preface to the Second 1989 Reprint

Pity. That was a good one. Can't remember how it was now.

Douglas Adams, Beijing, 1989

Preface to the Third 1989 Reprint

Did we make the point about all these words actually being real place names?

Douglas Adams, Mauritius, 1989

Preface to the Fourth 1989 Reprint

Yes.

John Lloyd, Lambeth, 1989

Preface to the First Edition of *The Deeper Meaning of Liff,* 1990

Well, there's not much we need to add to that then, really, is there?

Douglas Adams, John Lloyd, Sydney, 1990

Maps

A

Aith

Ardelve
Aird of Sleat
Ardslignish
Ardentinny

Aboyne
Aldclune

Articlave

Adrigole
Ardcrony
Aasleagh

Alltami
Ainderby Steeple
Ainderby Quernhow

Alltami
Aigburth
Ainsworth

Amlwch

Acle

Aberystwyth
Ahenny
Abercrave
Araglin
Aberbeeg

Amersham
Aynho
Adlestrop
Affpuddle
Abinger

Abert

Absecon, New Jersey
Acklins, Bahamas

Abalemma, Algeria
Abligo, Ethiopia
Abwong, Sudan
Addis Ababa, Ethiopia
Ambatolampy, Madagascar
Anjozorobe, Madagascar

Aalst, Belgium
Abruzzo, Italy
Albacete, Spain
Alcoy, Spain
Ampus, France
Aubusson, France

Ashdod, Isreal
Anantnag, Kashmir

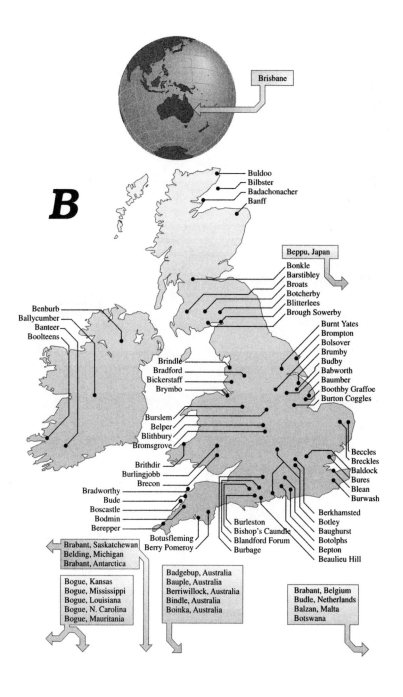

B

Brisbane

Buldoo
Bilbster
Badachonacher
Banff

Beppu, Japan

Bonkle
Barstibley
Broats
Botcherby
Blitterlees
Brough Sowerby

Benburb
Ballycumber
Banteer
Boolteens

Burnt Yates
Brompton
Bolsover
Brumby
Budby
Babworth
Baumber
Boothby Graffoe
Burton Coggles

Brindle
Bradford
Bickerstaff
Brymbo

Burslem
Belper
Blithbury
Bromsgrove

Beccles
Breckles
Baldock
Bures
Blean
Burwash

Brithdir
Burlingjobb
Brecon

Bradworthy
Bude
Boscastle
Bodmin
Berepper

Berkhamsted
Botley
Baughurst
Botolphs
Bepton
Beaulieu Hill

Burleston
Bishop's Caundle
Blandford Forum
Burbage

Botusfleming
Berry Pomeroy

Brabant, Saskatchewan
Belding, Michigan
Brabant, Antarctica

Badgebup, Australia
Bauple, Australia
Berriwillock, Australia
Bindle, Australia
Boinka, Australia

Brabant, Belgium
Budle, Netherlands
Balzan, Malta
Botswana

Bogue, Kansas
Bogue, Mississippi
Bogue, Louisiana
Bogue, N. Carolina
Bogue, Mauritania

C

Cadomin, Alberta
Cresbard, S. Dakota
Clingman's Dome, Tennessee
Canudos, Brazil
Chimbote, Peru

Corriemoillie
Cromarty
Corrievorrie
Clathy
Corriemuchloch
Crail
Corstorphine
Climpy
Coilantogle
Clackmannan
Caarnduncan
Corriecravie
Corriedoo
Cannock Chase
Clixby
Cotterstock
Clenchwarton
Condover
Clun
Cong Clabby Clonmult
Corfe
Chenies
Cranleigh
Chipping
Ongar
Camer

Dorchester, New Brunswick

Delaware, New York

Delaware, Ohio

Delaware, New Jersey

Delaware, Pennsylvania

Delaware, Delaware

Dunbar, W. Virginia

Dorchester, N.W. Territories

Dorchester, Wisconsin

Des Moines, Iowa

Dinsdale, Iowa

Duluth, Minnesota

Delaware, Kansas

Duluth, Olkahoma

Dunbar, Nebraska

Des Moines, New Mexico

Dunster, British Colombia

Dunbar, Alaska

Dunbar, Wisconsin

Dorchester, Nebraska

Dunbar, Utah

East Wittering Epworth
Edgbaston Eriboll
Elgin Esher
Elstrickle Escendine
Emsworth
Epsom

Elgin Exeter
Elgin Exeter
Elgin Exeter
Elgin Exeter Ely
Elgin Exeter Ely
Elgin Exeter Ely
Elgin Exeter
Elgin Exeter

Emmclaw Esterhazy

EUPHRATES

Epping

Ely

f

Frosses

Fiunary
Flodigarry
Foindle
Forsinain
Fladderbister

Foffarty

Farrancassidy

Flimby

Finuge

Farnham

Farduckmanton

Frolesworth
Fring

Framlingham

Farnham
Fovant
Fritham
Frimley
Fulking
Farnham
Frant
Frating Green

Farnham

Fraddam Fentonadle

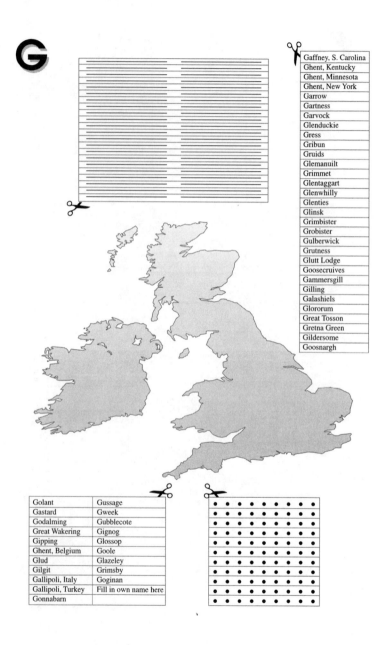

G

Gaffney, S. Carolina
Ghent, Kentucky
Ghent, Minnesota
Ghent, New York
Garrow
Gartness
Garvock
Glenduckie
Gress
Gribun
Gruids
Glemanuilt
Grimmet
Glentaggart
Glenwhilly
Glenties
Glinsk
Grimbister
Grobister
Gulberwick
Grutness
Glutt Lodge
Goosecruives
Gammersgill
Gilling
Galashiels
Glororum
Great Tosson
Gretna Green
Gildersome
Goosnargh

Golant	Gussage
Gastard	Gweek
Godalming	Gubblecote
Great Wakering	Gignog
Gipping	Glossop
Ghent, Belgium	Goole
Glud	Glazeley
Gilgit	Grimsby
Gallipoli, Italy	Goginan
Gallipoli, Turkey	Fill in own name here
Gonnabarn	

h

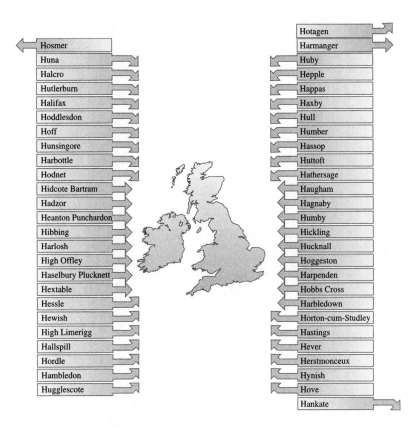

Hotagen

Harmanger

Hosmer

Huna

Halcro

Hutlerburn

Halifax

Hoddlesdon

Hoff

Hunsingore

Harbottle

Hodnet

Hidcote Bartram

Hadzor

Heanton Punchardon

Hibbing

Harlosh

High Offley

Haselbury Plucknett

Hextable

Hessle

Hewish

High Limerigg

Hallspill

Hordle

Hambledon

Hugglescote

Huby

Hepple

Happas

Haxby

Hull

Humber

Hassop

Huttoft

Hathersage

Haugham

Hagnaby

Humby

Hickling

Hucknall

Hoggeston

Harpenden

Hobbs Cross

Harbledown

Horton-cum-Studley

Hastings

Hever

Herstmonceux

Hynish

Hove

Hankate

i

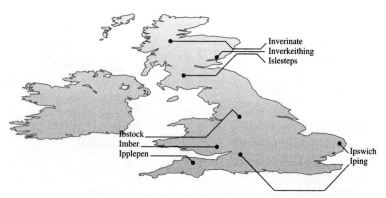

Inverinate
Inverkeithing
Islesteps

Ibstock
Imber
Ipplepen

Ipswich
Iping

J

Joliette, N. Dakota
Joplin, Missouri

Jubones, Ecuador

Jurby
Jawcraig
Jarrow

Jalingo, Nigeria
Jawf, Saudi Arabia
Jawf, Libya
Jawf, Yemen
Jid, Iraq
Jofane, Mozambique
Juwain, Afghanistan

K

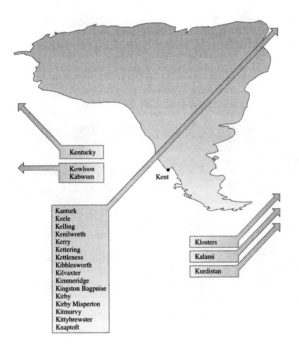

Kentucky

Kowloon
Kabwum

Kent

Kanturk
Keele
Kelling
Kenilworth
Kerry
Kettering
Kettleness
Kibblesworth
Kilvaxter
Kimmeridge
Kingston Bagpuise
Kirby
Kirby Misperton
Kitmurvy
Kittybrewster
Knaptoft

Klosters

Kalami

Kurdistan

L

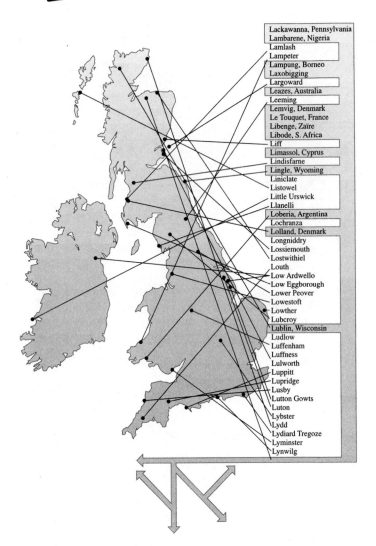

Lackawanna, Pennsylvania
Lambarene, Nigeria
Lamlash
Lampeter
Lampung, Borneo
Laxobigging
Largoward
Leazes, Australia
Leeming
Lemvig, Denmark
Le Touquet, France
Libenge, Zaïre
Libode, S. Africa
Liff
Limassol, Cyprus
Lindisfarne
Lingle, Wyoming
Liniclate
Listowel
Little Urswick
Llanelli
Loberia, Argentina
Lochranza
Lolland, Denmark
Longniddry
Lossiemouth
Lostwithiel
Louth
Low Ardwello
Low Eggborough
Lower Peover
Lowestoft
Lowther
Lubcroy
Lublin, Wisconsin
Ludlow
Luffenham
Luffness
Lulworth
Luppitt
Lupridge
Lusby
Lutton Gowts
Luton
Lybster
Lydd
Lydiard Tregoze
Lyminster
Lynwilg

M

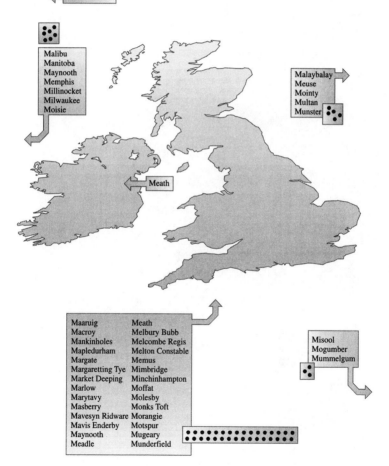

Massachusetts

Malibu
Manitoba
Maynooth
Memphis
Millinocket
Milwaukee
Moisie

Malaybalay
Meuse
Mointy
Multan
Munster

Meath

Maaruig	Meath
Macroy	Melbury Bubb
Mankinholes	Melcombe Regis
Mapledurham	Melton Constable
Margate	Memus
Margaretting Tye	Mimbridge
Market Deeping	Minchinhampton
Marlow	Moffat
Marytavy	Molesby
Masberry	Monks Toft
Mavesyn Ridware	Morangie
Mavis Enderby	Motspur
Maynooth	Mugeary
Meadle	Munderfield

Misool
Mogumber
Mummelgum

N

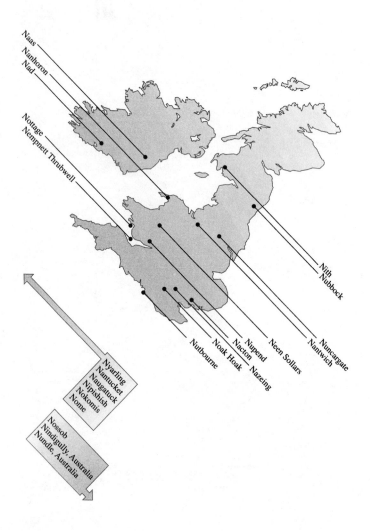

Naas
Nanboron
Nad

Nottage
Nempnett Thrubwell

Nith
Nubbock

Nuncargate
Nantwich

Nutbourne
Noak Hoak
Nacton
Nazeing
Nupend
Neen Sollars

Nyarling
Nantucket
Naugatuck
Nipishish
Nokomis
Nome

Nossob
Nindigully Australia
Nundle, Australia

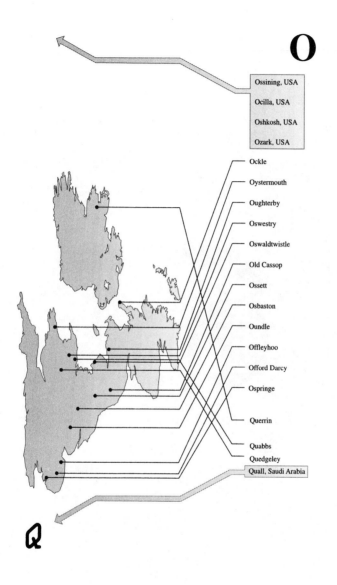

O

Ossining, USA

Ocilla, USA

Oshkosh, USA

Ozark, USA

Ockle

Oystermouth

Oughterby

Oswestry

Oswaldtwistle

Old Cassop

Ossett

Osbaston

Oundle

Offleyhoo

Offord Darcy

Ospringe

Querrin

Quabbs

Quedgeley

Quall, Saudi Arabia

Q

P

R

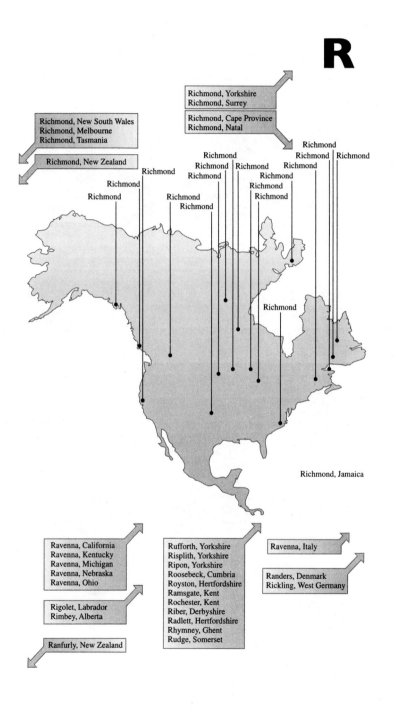

Richmond, Yorkshire
Richmond, Surrey

Richmond, Cape Province
Richmond, Natal

Richmond, New South Wales
Richmond, Melbourne
Richmond, Tasmania

Richmond, New Zealand

Richmond

Richmond
Richmond

Richmond

Richmond
Richmond

Richmond
Richmond

Richmond
Richmond

Richmond
Richmond

Richmond
Richmond Richmond
Richmond

Richmond

Richmond, Jamaica

Ravenna, California
Ravenna, Kentucky
Ravenna, Michigan
Ravenna, Nebraska
Ravenna, Ohio

Rigolet, Labrador
Rimbey, Alberta

Ranfurly, New Zealand

Rufforth, Yorkshire
Risplith, Yorkshire
Ripon, Yorkshire
Roosebeck, Cumbria
Royston, Hertfordshire
Ramsgate, Kent
Rochester, Kent
Riber, Derbyshire
Radlett, Hertfordshire
Rhymney, Ghent
Rudge, Somerset

Ravenna, Italy

Randers, Denmark
Rickling, West Germany

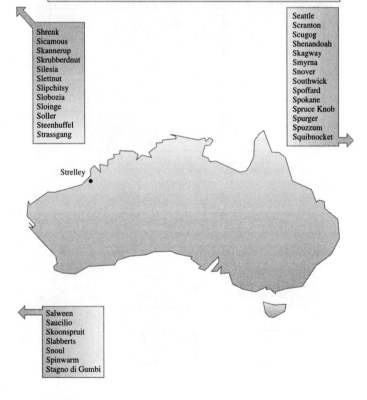

S

Sadberge	Screggan	Sidcup	Slumbay	Stebbing
Saffron Walden	Scremby	Sigglesthorne	Smarden	Stelling Minnis
Samalaman	Scridain	Silloth	Smearisary	Stibb
Satterthwaite	Scroggs	Simprim	Smisby	Stibbard
Savernake	Scronkey	Sittingbourne	Sneem	Stody
Scackleton	Scullet	Skegness	Snitter	Stoke Poges
Scamblesby	Scurlage	Skellister	Snittersfield	Stowting
Scethrog	Shalunt	Skellow	Snitterby	Strubby
Sconser	Shanklin	Skenfrith	Solent	Stutton
Scopwick	Sheepy Magna	Sketty	Sompting	Sturry
Scorrier	Shepper	Skibbereen	Sotterly	Suckley Knowl
Scosthrop	Shifnal	Skulamus	Spiddle	Surby
Scrabby	Shimpling	Sligo	Spittle Glenshee	Sutton and Cheam
Scrabster	Shirmers	Slogarie	Spofforth	Swaffham Bulbeck
Scramoge	Shoeburyness	Sloothby	Spreakley	Swanage
Scraptoft	Shottle	Slubbery	Sproston Green	Swanibost
Screeb	Shrivenham	Sluggan	Staplow	Swefling
				Symonds's Yat

Seattle
Scranton
Scugog
Shenandoah
Skagway
Smyrna
Snover
Southwick
Spoffard
Spokane
Spruce Knob
Spurger
Spuzzum
Squibnocket

Shrenk
Sicamous
Skannerup
Skrubberdnut
Silesia
Slettnut
Slipchitsy
Slobozia
Sloinge
Soller
Steenhuffel
Strassgang

Strelley

Salween
Saucilio
Skoonspruit
Slabberts
Snoul
Spinwarm
Stagno di Gumbi

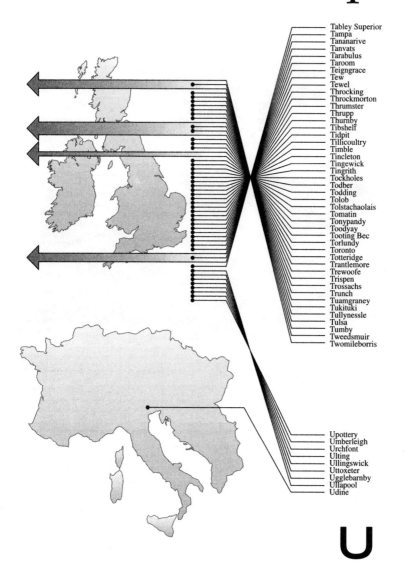

T

Tabley Superior
Tampa
Tananarive
Tanvats
Tarabulus
Taroom
Teigngrace
Tew
Tewel
Throcking
Throckmorton
Thrumster
Thrupp
Thurnby
Tibshelf
Tidpit
Tillicoultry
Timble
Tincleton
Tingewick
Tingrith
Tockholes
Todber
Todding
Tolob
Tolstachaolais
Tomatin
Tonypandy
Toodyay
Tooting Bec
Torlundy
Toronto
Totteridge
Trantlemore
Trewoofe
Trispen
Trossachs
Trunch
Tuamgraney
Tukituki
Tullynessle
Tulsa
Tumby
Tweedsmuir
Twomileborris

Upottery
Umberleigh
Urchfont
Ulting
Ullingswick
Uttoxeter
Ugglebarnby
Ullapool
Udine

U

W

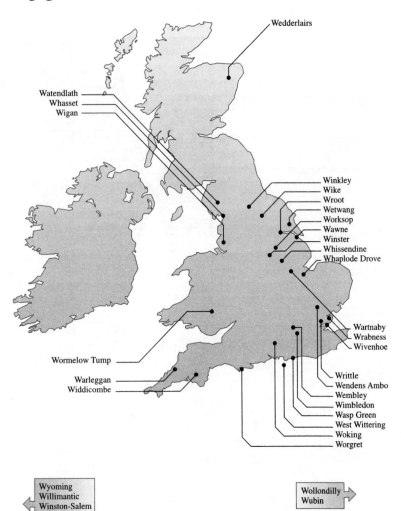

Wedderlairs

Watendlath
Whasset
Wigan

Winkley
Wike
Wroot
Wetwang
Worksop
Wawne
Winster
Whissendine
Whaplode Drove

Wartnaby
Wrabness
Wivenhoe

Wormelow Tump

Warleggan
Widdicombe

Writtle
Wendens Ambo
Wembley
Wimbledon
Wasp Green
West Wittering
Woking
Worgret

Wyoming
Willimantic
Winston-Salem
Waccamaw

Wollondilly
Wubin

V Y Z

HOW **t**O **P**RONOUNCE *the* **P**HO**N**E**T**IC **B**ITS

VOW**E**Ls

A: should be pronounced like the "a" in "gr<u>a</u>b"
> *except for:*
> ah: as in "f<u>a</u>ther"
> air: as in "h<u>ai</u>ry"
> ar: as in "c<u>ar</u>"
> aw: as in "<u>aw</u>ful"
> ay: as in "d<u>ay</u>"

E: should be pronounced like the short "e" in "g<u>e</u>t"
> *except for:*
> ee: as in "b<u>ee</u>n"
> er: short "er" sound as at the end of "moth<u>er</u>"
> ew: long "you" sound as at the front of "<u>U</u>ganda"

I: is short as in "ant<u>i</u>d<u>i</u>sestabl<u>i</u>shmentar<u>i</u>anism"
> igh: represents the long "i" as in "s<u>igh</u>"
> *Where "igh" would look completely silly, a long "i" between two consonants is represented by "y." Thus: FIREFIGHTERS is not rendered as FIGHR-FIGH-ters, but as FYR-FYT-erz, which is much better.*

O: is usually short as in "p<u>o</u>t"
> *except for:*
> oh: as in "z<u>o</u>ne"
> oo: as in "f<u>oo</u>d"
> oy: as in "b<u>oy</u>"

U: "u" sounds are rendered by the short "u" in "f<u>u</u>n"

except for:

ul: sort of swallowed like the "le" sound in "fidd<u>le</u>"

ur: longer "er" than in "mother," more like in "Ben-H<u>ur</u>"

uu: like the long "u" as in "m<u>oo</u>se"

ew: like the even longer "u" in "f<u>oo</u>d"

ou: like the interminably long "u" in "yo<u>uuuuuuuu</u> bastard"

Consonants

B: as in "<u>b</u>ug"

CH: as in "<u>ch</u>urch"

D: as in "<u>d</u>og"

DJ: like the "j" sound in "he<u>dg</u>e" (used when "j" on its own might be ambiguous)

F: as in "<u>f</u>at"

G: hard "g" as in "get"

GH: hard "g" as in "<u>gh</u>ost" (used when "g" on its own would be ambiguous)

The soft "g" as in "gin" is represented by "j" (see below).

H: as in "<u>h</u>ill"

J: as in "<u>j</u>eep"

K: as in "<u>k</u>ey"

KH: as in Scottish "lo<u>ch</u>"

L: as in Scottish "<u>l</u>och"

Good grief, there are a hell of a lot of these things to remember, aren't there?

M: as in "<u>m</u>int"

N: as in "k<u>n</u>ee"

P: as in "<u>p</u>an"

R: as in "<u>r</u>ug"

S: as in "<u>s</u>at"

T: as in "an<u>t</u>idises<u>t</u>ablishmen<u>t</u>arianism"

V: as in "pneumonoultramicroscopicsilico<u>v</u>olcanocoriosis"

W: as in "<u>w</u>ayzgoose"

Y: as in "wa<u>y</u>zgoose"

Z: as in "way<u>z</u>goose"[*]

ZH: like the "s" in "mea<u>s</u>ure" or the French "j" in "<u>j</u>e suis"

Double consonants (bb, ff, ll, ss, etc.) are used where single ones might be ambiguous. They have no other meaning

---

[*]**W**AYZGOOSE: A stubble-goose, an entertainment given to journeymen at the beginning of winter. (1731) *Oxford English Dictionary*. (Proof, if anyone should need it, that this book is a lot more use and only slightly less barmy than the *Oxford English Dictionary*).

A

Aalst (ay-AY-lst) *n.*
One who changes his name to be nearer the front.

Aasleagh (AHS-li-ukh) *n.*
A liqueur made only for drinking at the end of a revoltingly long bottle party when all the drinkable drink has been drunk.

Abalemma (AB-a-LEM-mah) *n.*
The agonizing situation in which there is only one possible decision but you still can't make it.

Aberbeeg (ab-a-BEEG) *vb.*
Of amateur actors, to adopt a Mexican accent when called upon to play any variety of foreigner (except Pakistanis—for whom a Welsh accent is considered sufficient).

Abercrave (ab-a-KRAYV) *vb.*
To desire strongly to swing from the pole on the footplate of a San Francisco cable car.

Abert (a-BERT) *vb.*
To change a baby's name at the last possible moment.

Aberystwyth (ab-a-RIST-with) *n.*
A nostalgic yearning which is in itself more pleasant than the thing being yearned for.

Abilene (AB-a-lene) *adj.*
Descriptive of the pleasing coolness on the reverse side of the pillow.

Abinger (AB-bin-jer) *n.*
One who washes everything except the frying pan, the cheese

grater and the saucepan in which the chocolate sauce has been made.

Abligo (AB-lig-goh) *n.*
One who prides himself on not even knowing what day of the week it is.

Aboyne (a-BOYN) *vb.*
To beat an expert at a game of skill by playing so appallingly that none of his clever tactics or strategies are of any use to him.

Abruzzo (a-BRUT-soh) *n.*
The worn patch of ground under a swing.

Absecon (AB-sek-on) *n.*
An annual conference held at the Dragonara Hotel, Leeds, for people who haven't got any other conferences to go to.

Abwong (AB-wong) *vb.*
To bounce cheerfully on a bed.

Acklins (AK-lins) *n.pl.*
The odd twinges you get in parts of your body when you scratch other parts.

Acle (AY-kul) *n.*
The rogue pin which shirtmakers conceal in a hidden fold of a new shirt. Its function is to stab you when you don the garment.

Addis Ababa (AD-is AB-ah-bah) *n.*
The torrent of incomprehensible gibberish which emanates from the loudspeakers on top of cars covered in stickers.

Adlestrop (AY-dul-strop) *n.*
The part of a suitcase which is designed to get snarled up on conveyor belts at airports. Some of the more modern adlestrop designs have a special "quick release" feature which enables the

case to flip open at this point and fling your underclothes into the
conveyor belt's gearing mechanism.

Adrigole (AD-ri-gohl) *n.*
The centerpiece of a merry-go-round on which the man with the
tickets stands unnervingly still.

Affcot (AF-kot) *n.*
The sort of fart you hope people will talk after.

Affpuddle (AF-pud-dul) *n.*
A puddle which is hidden under a pivoted paving stone. You only
know it's there when you step on the paving stone and the puddle
shoots up your leg.

Ahenny (ah-HEN-nee) *adj.*
The way people stand when examining other people's bookshelves.

Aigburth (AYG-berth) *n.*
Any piece of readily identifiable anatomy found among cooked
meat.

Ainderby Quernhow (AYN-der-bee-KWERN-how) *n.*
One who continually bemoans the loss of the word *gay* to the
English language, even though they had never used the word in any
context at all until they started complaining that they couldn't use
it anymore.

Ainderby Steeple (AYN-der-bee-STEE-pul) *n.*
One who asks you a question with the apparent motive of wanting
to hear your answer, but who cuts short your opening sentence by
leaning forward and saying, "And I'll tell you why I ask . . ." and
then talking solidly for the next hour.

Ainsworth (AYNZ-werth) *n.*
The length of time it takes to get served in a camera shop. Hence,
also, how long we will have to wait for the abolition of income tax
or the Second Coming.

Aird of Sleat (AYRD-uv-SLEET) *n.*

(Archaic) Ancient Scottish curse placed from afar on the stretch of land now occupied by Heathrow Airport.

Aith (AYTH) *n.*

The single bristle that sticks out sideways on a cheap paintbrush.

Albacete (AL-ba-seet) *n.*

A single surprisingly long hair growing in the middle of nowhere.

Albuquerque (AL-ba-KER-kee) *n.*

The shapeless squiggle which is utterly unlike your normal signature, but which is, nevertheless, all you are able to produce when asked formally to identify yourself. Muslims, whose religion forbids the making of graven images, use albuquerques to decorate their towels, menu cards and pajamas.

Alcoy (AL-koy) *adj.*

Wanting to be bullied into having another drink.

Aldclune (AWLD-kloon) *n.*

One who collects ten-year-old telephone directories.

Alltami (al-TAR-mee) *n.*

The ancient art of being able to balance the hot and cold shower taps.

Ambatolampy (am-BAHT-a-LAM-pee) *n.*

The bizarre assortment of objects collected by a sleepwalker.

Ambleside (AM-bul-side) *n.*

The talk given about the Facts of Life by a father to his son while walking in the garden on a Sunday afternoon.

Amersham (AM-a-sham) *n.*

The sneeze which tickles but never comes. (Thought to derive from London's Metropolitan Line tube station of the same name where rails always rattle but the train never arrives.)

Amlwch (AMLWCH*) *n.*
A British Rail sandwich which has been kept soft by being regularly washed and resealed in plastic wrap.

Ampus (AM-pus) *n.*
A lurid bruise which you can't remember getting.

Anantnag (AN-ant-nag) *vb.*
(Eskimo term) To bang your thumbs between the oars when rowing.

Anjozorobe (an-JOH-zoh-rohb) *n.*
A loose, colored garment someone brings you back from their travels which they honestly expect you to wear.

Araglin (a-RAG-lin) *n.*
(Archaic) The medieval practical joke played by young squires on a knight aspirant the afternoon he is due to start his vigil. As the knight arrives at the castle, the squires suddenly attempt to raise the drawbridge as the knight and his charger step on it.

Ardcrony (AHD-kroh-nee) *n.*
A remote acquaintance passed off as "a very good friend of mine" by someone trying to impress people.

Ardelve (AHR-delv) *n.*
To make a big display of searching all your pockets when approached by a charity collector.

Ardentinny (ahr-den-TIN-nee) *n.*
One who rubs his hands eagerly together when he sits down in a restaurant.

Ardslignish (ahd-SLIG-nish) *adj.*
Descriptive of the behavior of Scotch tape when you are tired.

*Good luck

ARDSLIGNISH

Articlave (ART-i-klayv) *n.*
A clever construction designed to give the illusion from the top of a double-decker bus that it is far too big for the road.

Ashdod (ASH-dod) *n.*
Any object against which a smoker habitually knocks out his pipe.

Aubusson (OH-be-son) *n.*
The hairstyle a girl adopts for a special occasion which suddenly gives you a sense of what she will look like in twenty years' time.

Aynho (AYN-hoh) *vb.*
Of waiters, never to have a pen.

B

Babworth (BAB-werth) *n.*
Something that justifies having a really good cry.

Badachonacher (bad-er-KON-er-ker) *n.*
An on-off relationship which never gets resolved.

Badgebup (BADJ-bup) *n.*
The splotch on a child's face where the ice cream cone has missed.

Baldock (BAWL-dok) *n.*
The sharp prong on top of a tree stump where the tree has snapped off before being completely sawed through.

Balemartine (BAYL-mar-TEEN) *n.*
The look which says, "Stop talking to that woman at once."

Ballycumber (ba-li-KUM-ber) *n.*
One of the six half-read books lying somewhere in your bed.

Balzan (bal-ZAN) *n.*
The noise of a trash can lid coming off in the middle of the night.

BARSTIBLEY

Banff (banf) *adj.*
> Pertaining to, or descriptive of, that kind of facial expression which is impossible to achieve except when having a passport photograph taken, which results in happas (*q.v.*).

Banteer (ban-TEER) *n.*
> (Archaic) A lusty and raucous old ballad sung after a particularly spectacular araglin (*q.v.*) has been pulled off.

Barstibley (bar-STIB-lee) *n.*
> A humorous device such as a china horse or small naked porcelain infant which jocular hosts use to piss water into your scotch with.

Bathel (BATH-ul) *vb.*
> To pretend to have read the book under discussion when in fact you've only seen the TV series.

Baughurst (BORG-herst) *n.*
> That kind of large, fierce, ugly woman who owns a small, fierce, ugly dog.

Baumber (BAWM-ber) *n.*
> A fitted elasticized bottom sheet which makes your mattress banana-shaped.

Bauple (BAW-pul) *n.*
> An indeterminate pustule which could be either a pimple or a bite.

Bealings (BEE-lingz) *pl. n.*
> (Archaic) The unsavory parts of a moat which a knight has to pour out of his armor after being the victim of an araglin (*q.v.*). In medieval Flanders, soup made from bealings was a very slightly sought-after delicacy.

Beaulieu Hill (BEW-lee-HILL) *n.*
> The optimum vantage point from which to view people undressing in the bedroom across the street.

Beccles (BEK-kuls) *pl. n.*
> The small bone buttons placed in bacon sandwiches by unemployed dentists.

Bedfont (BED-font) *n.*
> A lurching sensation in the pit of the stomach experienced at breakfast in a hotel, occasioned by the realization that it is about now that the chambermaid will have discovered the embarrassing stain on your bottom sheet.

Belding (BELD-ing) *n.*
> The technical name for a stallion after its first ball has been cut off. Any notice which reads "Beware of the Belding" should be taken very, very seriously.

Belper (BEL-per) *n.*
> A knob of someone else's chewing gum which you unexpectedly find your hand resting on under the passenger seat of your car or on somebody's thigh under their skirt.

Benburb (BEN-burb) *n.*
> Someone who aspires to work in a tollbooth.

Beppu (BEH-poo) *n.*
> The triumphant slamming shut of a book after reading the final page.

Bepton (BEP-ton) *n.*
> One who beams benignly after burping.

Berepper (beh-REP-pah) *n.*
> The irrevocable and sturdy fart released in the presence of royalty, which sounds like quite a small motorbike passing by (but not enough to be confused with one).

Berkhamsted (BUR-kum-sted) *n.*
> The massive three-course midmorning blow-out enjoyed by a dieter who has already done his or her slimming duty by having a spoonful of cottage cheese for breakfast.

Berriwillock (ber-ree-WIL-luk) *n.*
An unknown workmate who writes "All the best" on your going-away card.

Berry Pomeroy (ber-ree-POM-mer-roy) *n.*
1. The shape of a gourmet's lips.
2. The droplet of saliva which hangs from them.

Bickerstaff (BIK-er-stahf) *n.*
The person in an office whom everyone complains about in the pub. Many large corporations deliberately employ bickerstaffs in each department. For example, Sir Robert Maxwell was both Chairman and Chief Bickerstaff of the New York *Daily News*

Bilbster (BILB-ster) *n.*
A bauple (*q.v.*) so hideous and enormous that you have to cover it with a Band-Aid and pretend you've cut yourself shaving.

Bindle (BIN-dul) *vb.*
To slip foreign coins into a customer's change.

Bishop's Caundle (BISH-ups-KAWN-dul) *n.*
An opening gambit before a game of chess whereby the missing pieces are replaced by small ornaments from the mantelpiece.

Blandford Forum (BLAND-ferd-FOR-um) *n.*
Any middle-of-the-road radio chat show.

Blean (bleen) *n.*
Scientific measure of luminosity: 1 glimmer = 100,000 bleans. Usherettes' torches are designed to produce 2.5 and 4 bleans, enabling them to assist you in falling down stairs, treading on people or putting your hand into a Neapolitan tub when reaching for change.

Blithbury (BLITH-ber-ee) *n.*
A look someone gives you that indicates that he's much too drunk to have understood anything you've said to him in the last twenty minutes.

Blitterlees (BLIT-a-leez) *pl.n.*
The little slivers of bamboo picked off a cane chair by a nervous guest which litter the carpet beneath and tell the chair's owner that the whole piece of furniture is about to uncoil terribly and slowly until it resembles a giant pencil sharpening.

Bodmin (BOD-min) *n.*
The irrational and inevitable discrepancy between the amount pooled and the amount needed when a large group of people try to pay a bill together after a meal.

Bogue (bohg) *n.*
The expanse of skin that appears between the top of your socks and the bottom of your trousers when you sit down.
"The Duke of Ilford threw himself onto the chesterfield, brazenly displaying his bogues to the dowager Lady Ingatestone."
Barbara Cartland, *Come Soon, Strange Horseman*

Boinka (BOYN-ker) *n.*
The noise through the wall that tells you that the people next door enjoy a better sex life than you do.

Bolsover (BAWL-soh-ver) *n.*
One of those brown plastic trays with bumps, placed upside down in boxes of chocolates to make you think you're getting two layers.

Bonkle (BON-kul) *n.*
Of plumbing in old hotels, to make loud and unexplained noises in the night, particularly at about five o'clock in the morning.

Boolteens (BOOL-teenz) *pl.n.*
The small scatterings of foreign coins and pennies which inhabit dressing tables. Since they are never used and never thrown away, boolteens account for a significant drain on the world's money supply.

Boothby Graffoe (BOOTH-bi-GRAF-oh) *n.*
The man in the pub who slaps people on the back as if they were old friends, when in fact he has no friends, largely on account of this habit.

Boscastle (BOSS-kah-sul) *n.*
The huge pyramid of tin cans placed just inside the entrance to a supermarket.

Botcherby (BOTCH-er-bee) *n.*
The principle by which British roads are signposted.

Botley (BOT-lee) *n.*
The prominent stain on a man's trouser crotch seen on his return from the lavatory. A botley proper is caused by an accident with the faucets, and should not be confused with any stain caused by insufficient waggling of the willy (*q.v.* piddletrenthide).

Botolphs (BOT-olfs) *pl.n.*
Huge benign tumors that archdeacons and old chemistry teachers affect to wear on the sides of their noses.

Botswana (bot-SWAH-nah) *n.*
Something that is more fruitfully used for a purpose other than that for which it was designed. A fish knife used to lever open a stubborn can of luncheon meat is a fine example of a botswana.

Botusfleming (BOH-tus-flem-ing) *n.*
(Medical) A small, long-handled steel trowel used by surgeons to remove the contents of a patient's nostrils prior to a sinus operation.

Bozeman (BOZE-man) *n.*
One who spends all day loafing about near pedestrian crossings looking as if he's about to cross.

Brabant (brah-BANT) *adj.*
Very much inclined to see how far you can push someone.

Bradford (BRAD-ferd) *n.*
A schoolteacher's old hairy jacket, now severely discolored by chalk dust, ink, egg and the precipitations of unedifying chemical reactions.

Bradworthy (BRAD-wer-thee) *n.*
One who is skilled in the art of naming loaves.

Breckles (BREK-uls) *n.*
A disease of artificial plants.

Brecon (BREK-un) *n.*
The part of the toenail which is designed to snag on nylon sheets.

Brindle (BRIN-dul) *vb.*
To suddenly remember where it is you're meant to be going after you've already been driving for ten minutes.

Brisbane (BRIZ-bn) *n.*
A perfectly reasonable explanation. (Such as one offered by a person with a gurgling cough which has nothing to do with the fact that they smoke fifty cigarettes a day.)

Brithdir (BRITH-deer) *n.*
(Old Norse) The first day of winter on which your breath condenses in the air.

Broats (brohts) *pl.n.*
A pair of trousers with a career behind them. Broats are most commonly seen on elderly retired army officers. Originally the broats were part of their best suit back in the thirties; then in the fifties they were demoted and used for gardening. Recently, pensions not being what they were, the broats have been called out of retirement and reinstated as part of the best suit again.

Brompton (BROMP-tn) *n.*
A brompton is that which is said to have been committed when

you are convinced you are about to fart with a resounding trumpeting noise in a public place and all that actually slips out is a tiny "pfpt."

Bromsgrove (BROMZ-grohv) *n.*
Any urban environment containing a small amount of dog turd and about forty-five tons of bent steel pylon or a lump of concrete with holes claiming to be sculpture.

> "Oh, come my dear, and come with me
> And wander 'neath the bromsgrove tree"
> Betjeman

Brough Sowerby (BRUF SOW-er-bee) *n.*
One who has been working at the same desk in the same office for fifteen years and has very much his own ideas about why he is continually passed over for promotion.

Brumby (BRUM-bee) *n.*
The fake antique plastic seal on a pretentious whiskey bottle.

Brymbo (BRIM-boh) *n.*
The single unappetizing bun left in a baker's shop after 4:00 P.M.

Budby (BUD-bee) *n.*
A nipple clearly defined through flimsy or wet material.

Bude (bewd) *n.*
A polite joke reserved for use in the presence of vicars.

Budle (BEW-dul) *vb.*
To fart underwater.

Buldoo (bul-DOO) *n.*
A virulent red-colored pus that generally accompanies clonmult (*q.v.*) and sadberge (*q.v.*).

Burbage (BUR-bidj) *n.*
The sound made by an elevator full of people all trying to breathe through their noses.

Bures (b'YOORZ) *n.*

(Medical) The scabs on knees and elbows formed by a compulsion to make love on cheap floormatting.

Burleston (BER-leh-ston) *n.*

That peculiarly tuneless humming and whistling adopted by people who are extremely angry.

Burlingjobb (BUR-ling-job) *n.*

(Archaic) A seventeenth-century crime by which excrement is thrown into the street from a ground-floor window.

Burnt Yates (BURNT-YAYTS) *pl. n.*

Condition to which yates (*q.v.*) will suddenly pass without apparent intervening period, after the spirit of the throckmorton (*q.v.*) has finally been summoned by incessant throcking (*q.v.*).

Bursledon (BUR-zl-dn) *n.*

The bluebottle fly one is too tired to get up and swat, but not tired enough to sleep through.

Burslem (BERZ-lem) *n.*

One who goes on talking at three o'clock in the morning after everyone else has gone to sleep. The principal habitat of burslems is Radio 2.

Burton Coggles (BUR-tn-KOG-uls) *pl. n.*

A bunch of keys found in a drawer whose purpose has long been forgotten, and which can therefore now be used only for dropping down people's backs as a cure for nosebleeds.

Burwash (BER-wash) *n.*

The pleasurable cool sloosh of puddle water over the toes of your rubber boots.

C

Caarnduncan (KARN-DUNK'n) *n.*
 The high-pitched and insistent cry of the young male human urging one of its peer group to do something dangerous on a cliff edge or piece of toxic waste ground.

Cadomin (KAD-oh-min) *n.*
 The ingredient in coffee creamer that rises to the surface as scum.

Cafu (KA-foo) *n.*
 The frustration of not being able to remember what an acronym stands for.

Cahors (ka-HAWRZ) *pl. n.*
 The rushes of emotion triggered by overheard snatches of an old song.

Cairo (KIGH-roh) *n.*
 The noise of a spinning hubcap coming to rest.

Calicut (KAL-i-kut) *adj.*
 Determined not to let someone see how much his inadvertent remark has hurt you.

Camer (KAY-muh) *n.*
 A poorly tossed caber.

Cannock Chase (KAN-uk CHAYS) *n.*
 In any box of After Eight Mints, there is always a large number of empty envelopes and no more than four or five actual mints. The cannock chase is the process by which, no matter which part of the

box you insert your fingers into, or how often, you will always extract most of the empty sachets before pinning down an actual mint, or "cannock."

The cannock chase also occurs with people who put their dead matches back in the matchbox, and then embarrass themselves at parties trying to light cigarettes with three-quarters of an inch of charcoal.

The term is also used to describe futile attempts to pursue unscrupulous advertising agencies that steal your ideas to sell chocolates with.

Canudos (kah-NEW-dos) *n.*
The desire of married couples to see their single friends pair off.

Chaling (CHAY-ling) *ptcpl. vb.*
Trying not to be driven up the wall by the opinions of someone whom circumstances will not allow you to argue with.

Cheb (cheb) *n.*
An embarrassing nickname by which a fourteen-year-old boy insists that he now wishes to be known.

Chenies (CHAY-neez) *pl. n.*
The last few sprigs or tassles of last Christmas's decorations you notice on the ceiling while lying on the sofa on an August afternoon.

Chicago (shi-KAH-goh) *n.*
The foul-smelling wind which precedes an underground train.

Chimbote (CHIM-boh-tay) *n.*
A newly fashionable ethnic stew which, however much everyone raves about it, seems to you to have rather a lot of fish heads in it.

Chimkent (CHIM-kent) *n.*
One whose life appears not to have moved on in any direction at all when you meet him again ten years later.

Chipping Ongar (CHIP-ing-ONG-er) *n.*

The disgust and embarrassment (or "ongar") felt by an observer in the presence of a person festooned with kirbies (*q.v.*), when they don't know them well enough to tell them to wipe them off. Invariably this ongar is accompanied by an involuntary staccato twitching of the leg (or "chipping").

Clabby (KLAB-bi) *adj.*

A clabby conversation is one struck up by a commissionaire or cleaning lady in order to avoid any further actual work. The opening gambit is usually designed to provoke the maximum onfusion, and therefore the longest possible clabby conversation. It is vitally important to learn the correct, or clixby (*q.v.*), response to a clabby gambit, and not to get trapped by a ditherington (*q.v.*). For instance, if confronted with a clabby gambit such as "Oh Mr. Smith, I didn't know you'd had your leg off, " the ditherington response is "I haven't . . . " whereas the clixby is "Good."

Clackavoid (KLAK-a-void) *n.*

The technical term for a single page of script from an Australian soap opera.

Clackmannan (klak-MAN'n) *n.*

The sound made by knocking over an elephant's-foot umbrella stand full of walking sticks.

Clathy (KLATH-i) *adj.*

Nervously indecisive about how safely to dispose of a dud light bulb.

Clenchwarton (KLENCH-war-ton) *n.*

(Archaic) One who assists an exorcist by squeezing whichever part of the possessed the exorcist deems useful.

Climpy (KLIM-pee) *adj.*

Allowing yourself to be persuaded to do something and pretending to be reluctant.

Clingman's Dome (KLING-manz DOHM) *n.*
The condition in which it becomes impossible to put on a tie correctly when in a hurry for an important meeting.

Clixby (KLIKS-bee) *adj.*
Politely rude. Briskly vague. Firmly uninformative.

Cloates Point (KLOHTS point) *n.*
The precise instant at which scrambled eggs are ready.

Clonmult (clon-MULT) *n.*
A yellow ooze usually found near secretions of buldoo (*q.v.*) and sadberge (*q.v.*).

Clovis (KLOH-vis) *n.*
One who actually looks forward to putting up the Christmas decorations in the office.

Clun (KLUN) *n.*
A leg which has gone to sleep and has to be hauled around after you.

Clunes (KLOONS) *pl. n.*
People who just won't go.

Coilantogle (KOY-lan-toh-gul) *n.*
(Vulg.) Long elasticated loop of snot which connects a pulled bogey to a nose.

Condover (KON-doh-ver) *n.*
One who is employed to stand about all day browsing through the magazine rack at a newsstand.

Cong (kong) *n.*
Strange-shaped metal utensil found at the back of the saucepan cupboard. Many authorities believe that congs provide conclusive proof of the existence of a now-extinct form of yellow vegetable which the Victorians used to boil mercilessly.

Coodardy (koo-DAH-dee) *adj.*

> Astounded at what you've just managed to get away with.

Corfe (kawf) *n.*

> An object which is almost totally indistinguishable from a newspaper, the one crucial difference being that it belongs to somebody else and is unaccountably more interesting than your own—which may otherwise appear to be in all respects identical. Though it is a rule of life that a train or other public place may contain any number of corfes but only one newspaper, it is quite possible to transform your own perfectly ordinary newspaper into a corfe by the simple expedient of letting someone else read it.

Corfu (kor-FOO) *n.*

> The dullest person you met during the course of your holiday. Also the only one who failed to understand that the exchanging of addresses at the end of a holiday is merely a social ritual and is absolutely not an invitation to phone you or turn up unannounced on your doorstep three months later.

Corriearklet (kor-ee-ARK-let) *n.*

> The moment at which two people, approaching from opposite ends of a long passageway, recognize each other and immediately pretend they haven't. This is to avoid the ghastly embarrassment of having to continue recognizing each other the whole length of the corridor.

Corriecravie (kor-ee-KRAY-vee) *n.*

> To avert the horrors of corrievorrie (*q.v.*), corriecravie is usually employed. This is the cowardly but highly skilled process by which both protagonists continue to approach while keeping up the pretense that they haven't noticed each other—by staring furiously at their feet, grimacing into a notebook or studying the walls closely as if in a mood of deep irritation.

Corriedoo (kor-ee-DOO) *n.*

> The crucial moment of false recognition in a long passageway

encounter. Though both people are perfectly well aware that the other is approaching, they must eventually pretend sudden recognition. They now look up with a glassy smile, as if having spotted each other for the first time (and are particularly delighted to have done so), shouting out, "Haaaaallllllloooo!" as if to say "Good grief!! You!! Here!! Of all people! Well, I never. Coo. Stap me vitals," etc.

Corriemoillie (kor-ee-MOY-lee) *n.*
The dreadful sinking sensation in a long passageway encounter when both protagonists immediately realize they have plumped for the corriedoo (*q.v.*) much too early, as they are still a good thirty yards apart. They were embarrassed by the pretense of corriecravie (*q.v.*) and decided to make use of the corriedoo because they felt silly. This was a mistake, as corrievorrie (*q.v.*) will make them seem far sillier.

Corriemuchloch (kor-ee-MUK-lok) *n.*
The kind of person who can make a complete mess of a simple job like walking down a corridor.

Corrievorrie (kor-ee-VOH-ree) *n.*
Corridor etiquette demands that once a corriedoo (*q.v.*) has been declared, corrievorrie must be employed. Both protagonists must now embellish their approach with an embarrassing combination of waving, grinning, making idiot faces, doing pirate impressions and waggling the head from side to side while holding the other person's eyes as the smile drips off their face, until, with great relief, they pass each other.

Corstorphine (kaw-STAWF-een) *n.*
A very short peremptory service held in monasteries prior to teatime to offer thanks for the benediction of digestive biscuits.

Cotterstock (KOT-er-stok) *n.*
A piece of wood used to stir paint and thereafter stored uselessly in a shed in perpetuity.

Cowcaddens (KOW-kad-enz) *pl. n.*
A set of twelve cowcaddens makes an ideal and completely baffling wedding gift.

Craboon (kra-BOON) *vb.*
To shout boisterously from a cliff.

CONG

Crail (krayl) *n.*
Crail is a common kind of rock or gravel found widely across the British Isles. Each individual stone (due to an as-yet-undiscovered gravitational property) is charged with "negative buoyancy." This means that no matter how much crail you remove from the garden, more of it will rise to the surface. Crail is much employed by the Royal Navy for making the paperweights and ashtrays used in submarines.

Cranleigh (KRAN-lee) *n.*
A mood of irrational irritation with everyone and everything.

Cresbard (KRESS-bard) *n.*
> The light working lunch which Ann Hathaway used to make for her husband.

Crieff (kreef) *vb.*
> To agree sycophantically with a taxi driver.

Cromarty (KROM-ar-tee) *n.*
> The brittle sludge which clings to the top of ketchup bottles and plastic tomatoes in nasty diners.

D

Dalderby (DAWL-dur-bee) *n.*
> A letter to the editor made meaningless because it refers to a previous letter you didn't read (see A. H. Hedgehope, July 3rd).

Dalfibble (DAL-fib-ul) *vb.*
> To spend large periods of your life looking for car keys.

Dallow (DAL-loh) *adj.*
> Perfectly content to stare at something for no particular reason.

Dalmilling (dal-MILL-ing) *ptcpl. vb.*
> Continually making small talk to someone who is trying to read a book.

Dalrymple (DAL-rim-pul) *n.*
> Dalrymples are the things you pay extra for on pieces of handmad

craftwork—the rough edges, the paint smudges and the holes in the glazing.

Damnaglaur (DAM-na-GLAW) *n.*
A certain facial expression of which actors are required to demonstrate their mastery before they are allowed to play Macbeth.

Darenth (DA-renth) *n.*
Measure = 0.0000176 mg. Defined as that amount of margarine capable of covering one hundred slices of bread to a depth of one molecule. This is the legal maximum allowed in sandwich bars in Greater London.

Darvel (DAHR-vil) *vb*
To hold out hope for a better invitation until the last possible moment.

Dattuck (DAT-uk) *n.*
One who performs drum solos on his knees.

Deal (deel) *n.*
The gummy substance found between damp toes.

Dean Funes (DEEN FEWNZ) *pl. n.*
Things that clergymen opine on that are none of their damn business.

Delaware (DEL-a-wair) *n.*
The hideous stuff on the shelves of a rented house.

Des Moines (de MOYN) *pl .n.*
The two little lines that come down from your nose.

Detchant (DEH-chant) *n.*
The part of the hymn (usually a few notes at the end of the verse) where the tune goes so high or low that you suddenly have to change octaves to accommodate it.

Deventer (de-VEN-ter) *n.*

A decision that's very hard to make because so little depends on it—like which way to walk around a park.

Dewlish (DEW-lish) *adj.*

(Of the hands and feet) Prunelike after an overlong bath.

Didcot (DID-kot) *n.*

The tiny oddly shaped bit of card which a ticket inspector cuts out of a ticket with his clipper for no apparent reason. It is a little-known fact that the confetti at Princess Margaret's wedding was made up of thousands of didcots collected by inspectors on the Royal Train.

Dillytop (DIL-ee-top) *n.*

The kind of bath plug which for some unaccountable reason is actually designed to sit on top of the hole rather than fit into it.

Dinder (DIN-der) *vb.*

To nod thoughtfully while someone gives you a long and complex set of directions which you know you're never going to remember.

Dinsdale (DINZ-dayl) *n.*

One who always plays "Chopsticks" on the piano.

Dipple (DIP-pul) *vb.*

To try to remove a sticky something from one hand with the other, thus causing it to get stuck to the other hand and eventually to anything else you try to remove it with.

Ditherington (DITH-er-ing-tn) *n.*

Sudden access of panic experienced by one who realizes that he is being drawn inexorably into a clabby (*q.v.*) conversation, *i.e.*, one he has no hope of enjoying, benefiting from or understanding.

Dobwalls (DOB-wawls) *pl. n.*

The now-hardboiled bits of nastiness which have to be picked off crockery by hand after it has been through a dishwasher.

Dockery (DOK-er-ee) *n.*
Facetious behavior adopted by an accused man in the mistaken belief that this will endear him to the judge.

Dogdyke (DOG-dyk) *vb.*
Of dog owners, to adopt the absurd pretense that the animal shitting in the gutter has nothing to do with them.

Dolgellau (dol-GEL-ow) *n.*
The clump, or cluster, of bored, quietly enraged, mildly embarrassed men waiting for their wives to come out of a changing room in a dress shop.

Dorchester (DAW-ches-ter) *n.*
Someone else's throaty cough which obscures the crucial part of the rather amusing remark you've just made.

Dorridge (DOR-ridj) *n.*
Technical term for one of the very lame excuses written in very small print on the side of packets of food or detergent powder to explain why there's hardly anything inside. Examples include "Contents may have settled in transit" and "To keep biscuits fresh, they have been individually wrapped in silver paper and cellophane and separated with corrugated lining, a cardboard flap and heavy industrial tires."

Draffan (DRAF-an) *n.*
An infuriating person who always manages to look much more dashing than anyone else by turning up unshaven and hung over at a formal party.

Drebley (DREB-li) *n.*
Name for a shop which is supposed to be witty but is in fact wearisome, *e.g.*, "The Frock Exchange," "Hair Apparent," etc.

Droitwich (DROYT-wich) *n.*

A street dance. The two partners approach from opposite directions and try politely to get out of each other's way. They step to the left, step to the right, apologize, step to the left again, bump into each other and repeat as often as unnecessary.

Drumsna (DRUMZ-ner) *n.*

The earthquake that occurs when a character in a cartoon runs into a wall.

Dubbo (DUB-oh) *n.*

The bruise or callus on the shoulder of someone who has been knighted unnecessarily often.

Dubuque (de-BEWK) *n.*

A look given by a superior person to someone who has arrived wearing the wrong sort of shoes.

Duddo (DUD-doh) *n.*

The most deformed potato in any given collection of potatoes.

Dufton (DUF-tn) *n.*

The last page of a document that you always leave facedown in the photocopier and have to go and retrieve later.

Duggleby (DUG-ul-bee) *n.*

The person in front of you in the supermarket queue who has just unloaded a bulging shopping cart onto the conveyor belt and is now in the process of trying to work out which pocket he left his checkbook in, and indeed which pair of trousers.

Duleek (doo-LEEK) *n.*

Sudden realization, as you lie in bed waiting for the alarm to go off, that it should have gone off an hour ago.

Duluth (de-LOOTH) *adj.*

The smell of a taxi out of which people have just got.

Dunbar (dun-BAR) *n.*

A highly specialized fiscal term used solely by turnstile operatives at the zoo. It refers to the variable amount of increase in the gate takings on a Sunday afternoon, caused by persons going to the zoo because they are in love and believe that the feeling of romance will be somehow enhanced by the smell of panther sweat and rank incontinence in the reptile house.

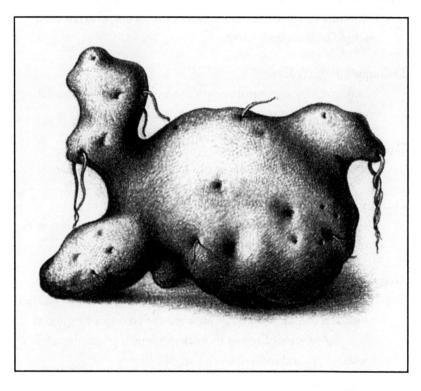

DUDDO

Dunboyne (dun-BOYN) *n.*
The realization that the train you have patiently watched pulling out of the station was the one you were meant to be on.

Duncraggon (DUN-KRAG-en) *n.*
The name of Charles Bronson's retirement cottage.

Dungeness (DUN-jen-ESS) *n.*
The uneasy feeling that the plastic handles of the overloaded supermarket bag you are carrying are getting steadily longer.

Dunino (DUN-ee-noh) *n.*
Someone who always wants to do whatever you want to do.

Dunolly (dun-OLL-ee) *n.*
An improvised umbrella.

Dunster (DUN-ster) *n.*
A small child hired to bounce at dawn on the occupants of the spare bedroom in order to save on tea and alarm clocks.

Duntish (DUN-tish) *adj.*
Mentally incapacitated by a severe hangover.

Eads (EEDZ) *pl. n.*
The sludgy bits in the bottom of a trash can, underneath the actual trash can liner.

Eakring (EE-kring) *ptcpl. vb.*
Wondering what to do next when you've just stormed out of something.

East Wittering (eest WIT-er-ing) *n.*
The same as West Wittering (*q.v.*), only it's you they're trying to get away from.

Edgbaston (EDJ-bas-tn) *n.*
The spare seat cushion carried by a London bus, which is placed against the rear bumper when the driver wishes to indicate that the bus has broken down.

Elgin (EL-ghin) *adj.*
Thin and haggard as a result of strenuously trying to get healthy.

Elsrickle (ELZ-rik-ul) *n.*
A bead of sweat which runs down your bottom cleavage.

Ely (EE-le) *n.*
The first, tiniest inkling you get that something, somewhere, has gone terribly wrong.

Emsworth (EMZ-werth) *n.*
Measure of time and noiselessness defined as the moment between the doors of an elevator closing and its beginning to move. Scientists believe we spend up to one-fifth of our lives in elevators.

Enumclaw (EEN-um-klaw) *n.*
One of the initiation rituals of the Freemasons which they are no longer allowed to do.

Epping (EP-ing) *ptcpl. vb.*
The futile movements of forefingers and eyebrows used when failing to attract the attention of waiters and bartenders.

Epsom (EP-sum) *n.*
An entry in a diary (such as a date or a set of initials) or a name and address in your address book, which you haven't the faintest idea what it's doing there.

Epworth (EP-worth) *n.*
The precise value of the usefulness of epping (*q.v.*). It is a little-known fact that an earlier draft of Clark Gable's final line of the film *Gone With the Wind* had him saying, "Frankly, my dear, I don't give an epworth," the line being eventually changed on the grounds that it might not be understood in Iowa, or indeed anywhere.

Eriboll (EH-ri-bol) *n.*
A brown bubble of cheese containing gaseous matter which grows on Welsh rarebit. It was Sir Alexander Fleming's study of eribolls that led, indirectly, to his discovery of the fact that he didn't like Welsh rarebit much.

Esher (EESH-ah) *n.*
One of those who push taps installed in public washrooms enabling the user to wash his trousers without actually getting into the basin. The most powerful esher of recent years was "damped down" by Red Adair after an incredible sixty-eight days' fight in Grand Central Station.

Essendine (ESS-en-dighn) *n.*
Long, slow sigh emitted by a fake leather armchair when sat on.

Esterhazy (EST-er-hay-zee) *adj.*
(Medical term) Suffering from selective memory loss. The virus causing this condition is thought to breed in the air-conditioning system of the White House.

Euphrates (yew-FRAY-teez) *n.*
The bullshit with which a chairman introduces a guest speaker.

Ewelme (yewlm) *n.*
The smile bestowed on you by an airline hostess.

Exeter (EKS-et-er) *n.*
All light household and electrical goods contain a number of vital components plus at least one exeter. If you've just mended a fuse, changed a bulb or fixed a blender, the exeter is the small plastic piece left over which means you have to undo everything and start all over again.

ELSRICKLE

Falster (FAWL-ster) *n.*
A long-winded, dishonest and completely incredible excuse used when the truth would have been perfectly acceptable.

Famagusta (FAR-mah-GOOS-ter) *n.*
The draft that whistles between two bottoms that refuse to touch.

Farduckmanton (FAR-duk-man-tn) *n.*
(Archaic) An ancient edict, mysteriously omitted from the
Domesday Book, requiring that the feeding of fowl on village
ponds should be carried out equitably.

Farnham (FAR-num) *n.*
The feeling that you get at about four o'clock in the afternoon
when you haven't got enough done.

Farrancassidy (FA-ran-CASS-i-dee) *n.*
A long and ultimately unsuccessful attempt to undo someone's bra.

Fentonadle (FEN-tun-ay-dul) *vb.*
To lay place settings with the knives and forks the wrong way
around.

Ferfer (FER-fer) *n.*
One who is very excited that he's had a better idea than the one
you've just suggested.

Finuge (fin-YEWJ) *vb.*
In any division of foodstuffs equally between several people, to
give yourself the extra slice left over.

Firebag (FYR-bag) *n.*
A remark intended to cue applause at a Republican
convention..

Fiunary (fi-YEWN-er-ee) *n.*
The safe place you put something and forget where it was.

Fladderbister (FLAD-er-bis-ter) *n.*
That part of a raincoat that trails out of a car after you've closed
the door on it.

Flagler (FLAY-gler) *n.*
Someone who always seems to disappear into shops when you're
walking along talking to him.

Flimby (FLIM-bee) *n.*
One of those irritating handleless slippery translucent plastic bags you get in supermarkets which, no matter how you hold them, always contrive to let something fall out.

Flodigarry (FLOD-ee-GAR-ee) *n.*
(Scots) An ankle-length oilskin worn by deep-sea herring fishermen in Nantucket and publicans in Glasgow.

Flums (flumz) *pl. n.*
Women who only talk to each other at parties.

Foffarty (FOF-er-tee) *adj.*
Unable to find the right moment to leave.

Foindle (FOYN-dul) *vb.*
To cut ahead in line very discreetly by working one's way up the line without being spotted..

Foping (FOH-ping) *ptcpl. vb.*
Refusing to say what it is you're looking so bloody wistful about.

Forsinain (FOR-sin-ayn) *n.*
(Archaic) The right of the lord of the manor to molest dwarves on their birthdays.

Fovant (FOV-unt) *n.*
A taxi driver's gesture, a raised hand pointed out of the window which purports to mean "Thank you" but actually means "Fuck off out of my way."

Fraddam (FRAD-dum) *n.*
The small awkward-shaped piece of cheese which remains after grating a large regular-shaped piece of cheese, and which enables you to grate your fingers.

Framlingham (FRAM-ling-um) *n.*
A kind of burglar alarm in common usage. It is cunningly designed so that it can ring at full volume in the street without apparently disturbing anyone.

Other types of framlinghams are burglar alarms fitted to business premises in residential areas, which go off as a matter of regular routine at 5:31 P.M. on a Friday evening and do not get turned off till 9:20 A.M. on Monday morning.

Frant (frant) *n.*
(Measure) The legal minimum distance between two trains on the District and Circle lines of the London Underground. A frant, which must be no less than 122 chains (or 8 leagues) long, is not connected in any way with the adjective "frantic," which comes to us by a completely different route (as indeed do the trains).

Frating Green (FRAY-ting GREEN) *adj.*
The shade of green which is supposed to make you feel comfortable in hospitals, industrious in schools and uneasy in police stations.

Fremantle (FREE-man-tul) *vb.*
To steal things not worth the bother of stealing. One steals cars, money and silver. Book matches, airline eye patches and individual pots of apricot jam are merely fremantled.

Frimley (FRIM-lee) *n.*
Exaggerated carefree saunter adopted by Charlie Chaplin as an immediate prelude to dropping down an open manhole.

Fring (fring) *n.*
The noise made by a light bulb which has just shone its last.

Fritham (FRIT-um) *n.*
A paragraph that you get stuck on in a book. The more often you read it through the less it means to you.

Frolesworth (FROHL-zwerth) *n.*
(Measure) The minimum time it is necessary to spend frowning in deep concentration at each picture in an art gallery in order that everyone else doesn't think you're a complete moron.

Frosses (FROSS-ez) *pl. n.*
The lecherous looks exchanged between sixteen-year-olds at a party given by someone's parents.

FAMAGUSTA

Frutal (FROOT-ul) *adj.*
Rather too eager to be cruel to be kind.

Fulking (FUL-king) *ptcpl. vb.*
Pretending not to be in when the carol singers come around.

Gaffney (GAF-nee) *n.*
Someone who deliberately misunderstands things for, he hopes, humorous effect.

Galashiels (gal-a-SHEELS) *pl. n.*
A form of particularly long sparse sideburns which are part of the mandatory turnout of British Rail guards.

Gallipoli (gal-LIP-oh-lee) *adj.*
Of the behavior of a bottom lip trying to spit out mouthwash after an injection at the dentist. Hence, loose, floppy, useless. "She went all Gallipoli in his arms."

—Noël Coward

Gammersgill (GAM-erz-gil) *n.*

Embarrassed stammer you emit when a voice answers the phone and you realize that you haven't the faintest recollection of who it is you've just rung.

Garrow (GAR-roh) *n.*

Narrow wiggly furrow left after pulling a hair off a painted surface.

Gartness (GART-ness) *n.*

The ability to say, "No, there's absolutely nothing the matter, what could possibly be the matter? And anyway, I don't want to discuss it," without moving your lips.

Garvock (GAR-vok) *n.*

The action of putting your finger in your cheek and flicking it out with a "pock" noise.

Gastard (GAS-terd) *n.*

Useful specially new-coined word for an illegitimate child (in order to distinguish it from someone who merely cuts you off on the highway, etc.).

Ghent (GHENT) *adj.*

Descriptive of the mood indicated by cartoonists by drawing a character's mouth as a wavy line.

Gignog (GIG-nog) *n.*

Someone who, through the injudicious application of alcohol, is now a great deal less funny than he thinks he is.

Gildersome (GIL-der-sum) *adj.*

Descriptive of a joke someone tells you that starts well but becomes so embellished in the telling that you start to weary of it after scarcely half an hour.

Gilgit (GIL-git) *n.*

Hidden sharply pointed object which stabs you in the cuticle when you reach into a small pot.

Gilling (GILL-ing) *n.*

The warm tingling you get in your feet when having a really good piddle.

Gipping (GIPP-ing) *ptcpl. vb.*

The fishlike opening and closing of the jaws seen among people who have recently been to the dentist and are puzzled as to whether their teeth have been put back the right way up.

Glasgow (GLAHZ-goh) *n.*

The feeling of infinite sadness engendered when walking through a place filled with happy people fifteen years younger than yourself. When experienced too frequently, it is likely to lead to an attack of trunch (*q.v.*).

Glassel (GLASS-ul) *n.*

A seaside pebble which was shiny and interesting when wet, and which is now a lump of rock, which children nevertheless insist on filling their suitcases with after the holiday.

Glazeley (GLAYZ-lee) *adj.*

The state of a barrister's flat greasy hair after wearing a wig all day.

Glemanuilt (GLEM-mon-ILT) *n.*

The kind of guilt that you'd completely forgotten about that comes roaring back on discovering an old letter in a cupboard.

Glenduckie (glen-DUK-ee) *n.*

Any Scottish actor who wears a cravat.

Glentaggart (glen-TAG-gert) *n.*

A particular kind of tartan hold-all, made exclusively under license for British Airways. When waiting to collect your luggage from an airport conveyor belt, you will notice that on the next conveyor belt there is always a single, solitary bag going round and round uncollected. This is a glentaggart, which has been placed there by the baggage-handling staff to take your mind off the fact that your own luggage will shortly be landing in Murmansk.

Glenties (GLEN-teez) *pl. n.*
Series of small steps by which someone who has made a serious tactical error in conversation or argument moves from complete disagreement to wholehearted agreement.

Glenwhilly (glen-WILL-i) *n.*
(Scots) A small tartan pouch worn beneath the kilt during the thistle harvest.

GLENWHILLY

Glinsk (glinsk) *n.*
A hat that politicians buy to go to Russia in.

Glororum (GLOR-ror-um) *n.*
One who takes pleasure in informing others about his bowel movements.

Glossop (GLOSS-up) *n.*
A rogue blob of food. Glossops, which are generally steaming hot and highly adhesive, invariably fall off your spoon and onto the surface of your host's highly polished antique rosewood dining

table. If this has not, or may not have, been noticed by the company present, swanage (q.v.) may be employed.

Glud (glud) *n.*
The pinkish mulch found in the bottom of a lady's handbag.

Glutt Lodge (GLUT LODJ) *n.*
The place where food can be stored after having a tooth extracted. Some Arabs can go without sustenance for up to six weeks on a full glutt lodge.

Godalming (GOD-ul-ming) *n.*
Wonderful rush of relief on discovering that the ely (q.v.) and the wembley (q.v.) were in fact false alarms.

Goginan (GOG-ee-nan) *n.*
The piece of adhesive tape on a nearsighted child's spectacles.

Golant (GOL-unt) *adj.*
Blank, sly and faintly embarrassed. Pertaining to the expression seen on the face of someone who has clearly forgotten your name.

Gonnabarn (GON-er-barn) *n.*
An afternoon wasted on watching an old movie on TV.

Goole (gool) *n.*
The puddle on the bar into which the barman puts your change.

Goosecruives (GOOS-crives) *pl. n.*
(Archaic) A pair of wooden trousers worn by poultry keepers in the Middle Ages.

Goosnargh (GOO-snarg) *n.*
Something left over from preparing or eating a meal, which you store in the fridge despite the fact that you know full well that you will never ever use it.

Great Tosson (grayt TOSS-on) *n.*
A fat book containing four words and six cartoons which costs $20.00.

Great Wakering (grayt WAY-ker-ing) *ptcpl. vb.*
Panic which sets in when you badly need to go to the lavatory and cannot make up your mind about what book or magazine to take with you.

Greeley (GREE-lee) *n.*
Someone who continually annoys you by continually apologizing for annoying you.

Gress (gress) *vb.*
(Rare) To stick to the point during a family argument.

Gretna Green (GRET-nuh GREEN) *adj.*
A shade of green which makes you wish you'd painted whatever it was a different color.

Gribun (GREE-bun) *n.*
The person in a crisis who can always be relied on to make a good anecdote out of it.

Grimbister (GRIM-bis-ter) *n.*
Large body of cars on a highway all traveling at exactly the speed limit because one of them is a police car.

Grimmet (GRIM-et) *n.*
A small bush from which cartoon characters dangle over the edge of a cliff.

Grimsby (GRIMZ-bee) *n.*
A lump of something gristly and foul-tasting concealed in a mouthful of stew or pie. Grimsbies are sometimes merely the result of careless cookery, but more often they are placed there deliberately by Freemasons. Grimsbies can be purchased in bulk from any respectable Masonic butcher upon giving him the secret Masonic handbag. One is then placed in a guest's food to see if he knows the correct Masonic method of dealing with it.
This is as follows: Remove the grimsby carefully with the silver

tongs provided. Cross the room to your host, hopping on one leg, and ram the grimsby firmly up his nose, chanting, "Take that, you smug Masonic bastard."

Grinstead (GRIN-sted) *n.*
The state of a woman's clothing after she has been to powder her nose and has hitched up her tights over her skirt at the back, thus exposing her bottom, and has walked out without noticing it.

Grobister (GROH-bis-ter) *n.*
One who continually and publicly rearranges the position of his genitals.

Gruids (GREW-idz) *n.*
The only bits of an animal left after even the people who make sausage rolls have been at it.

Grutness (GRUT-ness) *n.*
The resolve with which the Queen sits through five days of Polynesian folk dancing.

Gubblecote (GUB-ul-koht) *n.*
Deformation of the palate caused by biting into too many Toblerones.

Guernsey (GERN-zee) *adj.*
Queasy but unbowed. The kind of feeling one gets when discovering a plastic compartment in a fridge in which things are growing, usually fertilized by copious quantities of goosnargh (*q.v.*).

Gulberwick (GUL-ber-wik) *n.*
The small particle that you always think you've got stuck in the back of your throat after you've been sick.

Gussage (GUSS-idj) *n.*
Dress-making talk.

Gweek (gweek) *n.*
A coat hanger recycled as a car aerial.

H

Hadweenzic (had-WEEN-zik) *adj.*
Resistant to tweezers.

Hadzor (HAD-zer) *n.*
A sharp instrument placed in the basin which makes it easier to cut yourself.

Hagnaby (HAG-nay-bee) *n.*
Someone who looked a lot more attractive in the disco than she does in your bed the next morning.

Halcro (HAL-kroh) *n.*
An adhesive cloth designed to fasten baby clothes together. Thousands of tiny pieces of jam "hook" on to thousands of pieces of dribble, enabling the cloth to become "sticky."

Halifax (HAL-i-faks) *n.*
The green synthetic Astroturf on which greengrocers display their vegetables.

Hallspill (HAWL-spil) *n.*
The name for the adventurous party-goers who don't spend the whole time in the kitchen.

Hambledon (HAM-bul-den) *n.*
The sound of a single-engined aircraft flying by, heard while lying in a meadow in New England, which somehow concentrates the silence and sense of space and timelessness and leaves one with the feeling of something or other.

Hankate (HAN-kayt) *adj.*
Congenitally incapable of ever having a paper tissue.

Happas (HAPP-as) *n.*
The amusement caused by passport photos.

Happle (HAP-pul) *vb.*
To annoy people by finishing their sentences for them and then telling them what they really meant to say.

Harbledown (HAR-bul-down) *vb.*
To maneuver a double mattress down a winding staircase.

Harbottle (HAR-bot-ul) *n.*
A particular kind of fly which lives inside double glazing.

Harlosh (HAR-losh) *vb.*
To redistribute the hot water in a bath.

Harmanger (HAR-man-jer) *n.*
The person who takes the blame while the manager you demanded to see hides in his office.

Harpenden (HAR-pen-dn) *n.*
The coda to a phone conversation, consisting of about eight exchanges, by which people try gracefully to get off the line.

Haselbury Plucknett (HAY-zul-bree PLUK-net) *n.*
A mechanical device for cleaning combs invented during the industrial revolution at the same time as Arkwright's Spinning Jenny, but which didn't catch on in the same way.

Hassop (HAS-sup) *n.*
The pocket down the back of an armchair used for storing pennies and bits of Lego.

Hastings (HAYS-tings) *pl. n.*
Things said on the spur of the moment to explain to someone who unexpectedly comes into a room precisely what it is you are doing.

Hathersage (HATH-a-saydj) *n.*
The tiny snippets of beard which coat the inside of a washbasin after shaving in it.

Haugham (hawm) *n.*
> One who loudly informs other diners in a restaurant what kind of man he is by calling the chef by his Christian name from the lobby.

Haxby (HAKS-bee) *n.*
> Any gardening implement found in a tool shed whose exact purpose is unclear.

HAXBY

Heanton Punchardon (HEEN-tn pun-CHARD'n) *n.*
> A violent argument that breaks out in the car on the way home from a party between a couple who have had to be polite to each other in company all evening.

Henstridge (HEN-stridj) *n.*
> A dried yellow substance found between the prongs of forks in restaurants.

Hepple (HEP-pul) *vb.*
To sculpt the contents of a sugar bowl.

Herstmonceux (HERST-mon-SUR) *n.*
The correct name for the gold medallion worn by someone who is in the habit of wearing his shirt open to the waist.

Hessle (HES-sul) *vb.*
To try to sort out which sleeve of a sweater is inside out when you're already halfway through putting it on.

Hever (HEE-vah) *n.*
The panic caused by half hearing a public-address system.

Hewish (HEW-ish) *adj.*
In a mood to swipe at vegetation with a stick.

Hextable (HEKS-tah-bul) *n.*
The record you find in someone else's collection which instantly tells you you could never go out with them.

Hibbing (HIB-bing) *n.*
The marks left on the outside breast pocket of a storekeeper's overall where he put away his pen and missed.

Hickling (HIK-ling) *ptcpl. vb.*
The practice of infuriating theatergoers by not only arriving late to a center-row seat, but also loudly apologizing to and patting each member of the audience in turn.

Hidcote Bartram (HID-koht BAR-tram) *n.*
To be caught in a hidcote bartram is to say a series of protracted and final good-byes to a group of people and then realize that you've left your hat behind.

High Limerigg (high LIME-rig) *n.*
The topmost tread of a staircase which disappears when you're climbing the stairs in darkness.

High Offley (high OFF-lee) *n.*
Goosnargh (*q.v.*) three weeks later.

Hobarris (hoh-BA-ris) *n.*
(Medical) A sperm which carries a high risk of becoming a bank manager.

Hobbs Cross (HOBZ CROS) *n.*
The awkward leaping maneuver a girl has to go through in bed in order to make him sleep on the wet patch.

Hoddlesdon (HOD-ulz-dn) *n.*
An "injured" footballer's limp back into the game which draws applause but doesn't fool anybody.

Hodnet (HOD-net) *n.*
The wooden safety platform supported by scaffolding around a building under construction from which the builders (at almost no personal risk) can drop pieces of cement on passersby.

Hoff (hoff) *vb.*
To deny indignantly something which is palpably true.

Hoggeston (HOG-us-tn) *n.*
The action of overshaking a pair of dice in a cup in the mistaken belief that this will affect the eventual outcome in your favor and not irritate everyone else.

Hordle (HAW-dul) *vb.*
To dissemble in a fruity manner, like William F. Buckley.

Horton-cum-Studley (HAWT'n kum STUD-lee) *n.*
The combination of little helpful grunts, nodding movements of the head, considerate smiles, upward frowns and serious pauses that a group of people join in making in trying to elicit the next pronouncement of somebody with a terrible stutter.

Hosmer (HOZ-mah) *vb.*
(Of a TV newsreader) To continue to stare impassively into the camera when it should have already switched to the sports report.

Hotagen (HOT-a-jen) *n.*
The aggressiveness with which a shop assistant sells you any piece of high technology which they don't understand themselves.

Hove (hohv) *adj.*
Descriptive of the expression seen on the face of one person in the presence of another who clearly isn't going to stop talking for a very long time.

Huby (HEW-bee) *n.*
A half erection large enough to be a publicly embarrassing bulge in the trousers, but not large enough to be of any use to anybody.

Hucknall (HUK-nul) *vb.*
To crouch upward, as in the movement a seated person's feet and legs make to allow a vacuum cleaner to pass beneath them.

Hugglescote (HUG-gulz-koht) *n.*
Someone who excitedly opens a letter that says, "You may already have won £10,000" on the outside.

Hull (hul) *adj.*
Descriptive of the smell of a weekend cottage.

Humber (HUM-bah) *vb.*
To move like the cheeks of a very fat person as his car goes over a cattle grid.

Humby (HUM-bee) *n.*
An erection that won't go down when a gentleman has to go to the lavatory in the middle of dallying with a lady.

Huna (HEW-nah) *n.*
The result of coming to the wrong decision.

Hunsingore (HUN-sin-gaw) *n.*
Medieval ceremonial brass horn with which the successful execution of an araglin (*q.v.*) is trumpeted from the castle battlements.

Hutlerburn (HUT-ler-bern) *n.*
(Archaic) A burn sustained as a result of the behavior of a clumsy hutler. (The precise duties of hutlers are now lost in the mists of history.)

Huttoft (HUT-oft) *n.*
The fibrous algae which grows in the dark, moist environment of trouser cuffs.

Hynish (HIGH-nish) *adj.*
Descriptive of the state of mind in which you might as well give up doing whatever it is you're trying to do because you'll only muck it up.

i

Ible (IGH-bull) *adj.*
Clever but lazy.

Ibstock (IBZ-tok) *n.*
Anything used to make a noise on a corrugated iron wall or chain-link fence by dragging it along the surface while walking past it. "Mr Bennett thoughtfully selected a stout ibstock and left the house."
—Jane Austen, *Pride and Prejudice*, II

Imber (IM-ber) *vb.*

To lean from side to side while watching a car chase in the cinema.

Inigonish (in-i-GOH-nish) *adj.*

Descriptive of the expression on the face of a dinner party guest which is meant to indicate huge enjoyment to the hosts and "time to go home, I think" to your partner. An inigonish is usually the prelude to a heanton punchardon *(q.v.)*.

Inverinate (in-VER-i-nayt) *vb.*

To spot that both people in a heated argument are talking complete rubbish.

Inverkeithing (in-ver-KEE-thing) *ptcpl. vb.*

Addressing someone by mumble because you can only remember the first letter of their name.

Iping (IGH-ping) *ptcpl. vb.*

The increasingly anxious shifting from leg to leg you go through when you are desperate to go to the lavatory and the person you are talking to keeps on remembering a few final things he wants to mention.

IPPLEPEN

Ipplepen (IP-pul-pen) *n.*
A useless writing implement made by taping six ballpoint pens together, which is supposed to make it easier to write one hundred lines.

Ipswich (IPS-wich) *n.*
The sound at the other end of the telephone which tells you that the automatic exchange is working very hard but is intending not actually to connect you this time, merely to let you know how difficult it is.

Islesteps (IGH-zul-steps) *pl. n.*
Cautious movements toward the bathroom in a strange house in the dark.

Jalingo (ja-LING-goh) *n.*
The alacrity with which a grimbister *(q.v.)* breaks up as soon as the police car turns off.

Jarrow (JA-roh) *adj.*
An agricultural device which, when towed behind a tractor, enables the farmer to spread his dung evenly across the width of the road.

Jawcraig (JAW-krayg) *n.*
(Medical) A massive facial spasm which is brought on by being told a really astounding piece of news. A mysterious attack of jawcraig affected forty thousand sheep in Wales in 1952.

Jawf (JAWF) *n.*
Conversation between two soccer hooligans on a train.

Jeffers (JEFF-erz) *pl. n.*
Persons who honestly believe that a business lunch is going to achieve anything.

Jid (JID) *n.*
The piece of paper on top of the jam inside the jam jar.

Jofane (jo-FAYN) *adj.*
In breach of the laws of joke telling, *e.g.*, giving away the punch line in advance.

Joliette (ZHO-lee-et) *n.*
(Old French) Polite word for a well-proportioned dog turd.

JURBY

Joplin (JOP-lin) *n.*
The material from which all the clothes in Woolworth's are made.

Jubones (JEW-bohnz) *pl. n.*
Awful things bought in Nairobi that never look good at home.

Jurby (JUR-bi) *n.*
A loose woolen garment reaching to the knees and with three or more armholes, knitted by the wearer's well-meaning but incompetent aunt.

Juwain (ju-WAYN) *adj.*
Only slightly relevant to the matter in hand.

K

Kabwum (KAB-wum) *n.*
The cutesy humming noise you make as you go to kiss someone on the cheek.

Kalami (kal-AH-mee) *n.*
The ancient Eastern art of being able to fold road maps properly.

Kanturk (kan-TERK) *n.*
An extremely intricate knot originally used for belaying the topgallant foresheets of a gaff-rigged China clipper, and now more commonly observed when trying to get an old kite out of the cupboard under the stairs.

Keele (keel) *n.*
The horrible smell caused by washing ashtrays.

Kelling (KEL-ling) *ptcpl. vb.*
The action of looking for something all over again in all the places you've already looked.

Kenilworth (KEN-nul-werth) *n.*
A measure. Defined as that proportion of a menu which the waiter speaks that you can actually remember.

Kent (kent) *adj.*
Politely determined not to help despite a violent urge to the contrary. Kent expressions are seen on the faces of people who are good at something watching someone else who can't do it at all.

Kentucky (ken-TUK-ee) *adj.*
Fitting exactly and satisfyingly. The cardboard box that slides neatly into a small space in a garage, or the last book which precisely fills a bookshelf, is said to fit "real nice and kentucky."

Kerry (KER-ri) *n.*
The small twist of skin which separates each sausage on a string.

Kettering (KET-er-ing) *n.*
The marks left on your bottom or thighs after sunbathing on a wicker chair.

Kettleness (KET-tul-nes) *adj.*
The quality of not being able to pee while being watched.

Kibblesworth (KIB-bulz-werth) *n.*
The footling amount of money by which the price of a given article in a shop is less than a sensible number, in the hope that at least one idiot will think it cheap. For instance, the kibblesworth on a pair of shoes priced at $19.99 is 1cent.

Kilvaxter (kil-VAKS-ter) *n.*
A pen kept in the desk tidy that never works.

Kimmeridge (KIM-er-idj) *n.*
The light breeze which blows through your armpit hair when you are stretched out sunbathing.

Kingston Bagpuise (KING-ston BAG-pweez) *n.*
A forty-year-old overweight man trying to commit suicide by jogging.

Kirby (KER-bee) *n.*
Small but repulsive piece of food prominently attached to a person's face or clothing; chipping ongar *(q.v.)*.
Kirby Misperton (KER-bee mis-PER-ton) n.
One who kindly attempts to wipe a kirby (q.v.) off another's face with a napkin, and then discovers it to be a wart or other permanent fixture, is said to have committed a "kirby misperton."

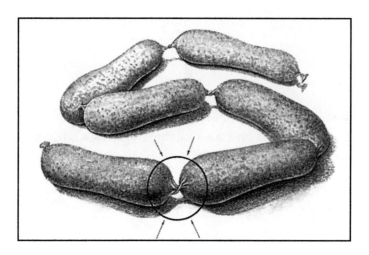

KERRY

Kitmurvy (kit-MER-vee) *n.*
Man who owns all the latest sporting gadgetry and clothing (golf cart, tee cosies, ventilated shoes, Gary Player autographed tracksuit top, American navy cap, mirror sunglasses) but is still only on his second golf lesson.

Kittybrewster (kit-ee BROO-ster) *n.*
The girl who always offers to make the tea.

Klosters (KLOHS-terz) *pl. n.*
The little blobs of dried urine on the rim of the bowl under the seat.

Knaptoft (NAP-toft) *n.*
The mysterious fluff placed in your pockets by dry-cleaning firms.

Kowloon (kow-LOON) *n.*
One who goes to an Indian restaurant and orders an omelette.

Kurdistan (KOOR-dis-TAHN) *n.*
Hard stare given by a husband to his wife when he notices a sharp increase in the number of times he answers the phone to be told, "Sorry, wrong number."

L

Lackawanna (LAK-ka-WAN-na) *n.*
The inability of a New York cabdriver to know where, for instance, Central Park is.

Lambarene (LAM-ba-reen) *adj.*
Feeling better for having put pajamas on.

Lamlash (LAM-lash) *n.*
The folder on hotel dressing tables full of astoundingly dull information.

Lampeter (LAM-pit-er) *n.*
The fifth member of a foursome.

Lampung (LAM-poong) *n.*
The daze which follows turning on the light in the middle of the night.

Largoward (LAH-goh-ord) *n.*
Motorists' name for the kind of pedestrian who stands beside a main road and waves on the traffic, as if it's his right of way.

Laxobigging (LAKS-oh-BIG-ing) *ptcpl. vb.*
Struggling to extrude an extremely large turd.

Le Touquet (lur TOO-kay) *n.*
A mere nothing, an unconsidered trifle, a negligible amount. Un touquet is often defined as the difference between the cost of a bottle of gin bought in a liquor store and one bought in a duty-free shop.

Leazes (LEE-zez) *pl. n.*
Irritating pains that your doctor tells you not to be so upset about.

Leeming (LEE-ming) *prtcpl. n.*
The business of making silly faces at babies.

Lemvig (LEM-vig) *n.*
A person who can be relied upon to be doing worse than you.

Libenge (LIGH-bendj) *n.*
Crystallized deposits of old cough mixture.

Libode (LIGH-bohd) *adj.*
Being undecided about whether or not you feel sexually attracted to someone.

Liff (lif) *n.*
A common object or experience for which no word yet exists.

Limassol (LIM-a-sol) *n.*
The correct name for one of those little paper umbrellas which come in cocktails with too much pineapple juice in them.

Lindisfarne (LIN-dis-farn) *adj.*
Descriptive of the pleasant smell of an empty biscuit tin.

Lingle (LING-gul) *vb.*
 To touch battery terminals with one's tongue.

Liniclate (LIN-i-klayt) *adj.*
 All stiff and achy in the morning and trying to remember why.

Listowel (LIS-towl) *n.*
 The small mat on the bar designed to be more absorbent than the bar, but not as absorbent as your elbows.

Little Urswick (LIT-ul ERZ-wik) *n.*
 The member of any class who most inclines the teacher toward the view that capital punishment should be introduced in schools.

Llanelli (khlan-EKHL-i) *adj.*
 Descriptive of the waggling movement of a person's hands when shaking water from them or warming up for a piece of workshop theater.

Loberia (lo-BEER-ee-ah) *n.*
 Unshakable belief that your ears stick out.

Lochranza (lokh-RAN-zah) *n.*
 The long unaccompanied wail in the middle of a Scottish folk song where the pipers nip round the corner for a couple of drinks.

Lolland (LOL-and) *n.*
 A person with a low threshold of boredom.

Longniddry (LONG-NID-ree) *n.*
 A droplet which persists in running out of your nose.

Lossiemouth (LOS-see-mowth) *n.*
 One of those middle-aged ladies with just a hint of a luxuriant handlebar mustache.

Lostwithiel (los-WITH-ee-ul) *n.*
 The deep and peaceful sleep you finally fall into two minutes before the alarm goes off.

Louth (LOWTH) *n.*

> The sort of man who wears loud check jackets, has a personalized tankard behind the bar and always gets served before you do.

Low Ardwello (LOH ard-WEL-low) *n.*

> Seductive remark made hopefully in the back of a taxi.

Low Eggborough (LOH EG-ber-ah) *n.*

> A quiet little unregarded man in glasses who is building a new kind of atomic bomb in his garden shed.

Lower Peover (LOH-er PEE-oh-ver) *n.*

> Common solution to the problem of a humby *(q.v.)*.

Lowestoft (LOH-es-toft) *n.*

> The correct name for "navel fluff."

Lowther (LOW-ther) *vb.*

> (Of a large group of people who have been to the cinema together) To stand aimlessly about on the pavement and argue about whether to go and eat either a Chinese meal nearby or an Indian meal at a restaurant which somebody says is very good but isn't certain where it is, or just go home, or have a Chinese meal nearby—until by the time agreement is reached everything is shut.

Lubcroy (LUB-kroy) *n.*

> The telltale little lump in the top of your swimming trunks which tells you you are going to have to spend half an hour with a safety pin trying to pull the drawstring out again.

Lublin (LUB-lin) *n.*

> The bit of somebody's body which their partner particularly likes.

Ludlow (LUD-loh) *n.*

> A wad of newspaper, folded table napkin or lump of cardboard put under a wobbly table or chair to make it stand up straight. It is perhaps not widely known that air ace Sir Douglas Bader used to

get about on an enormous pair of ludlows before he had his artificial legs fitted.

Luffenham (LUF-en-um) *n.*
Feeling you get when the pubs aren't going to be open for another forty-five minutes and the luffness *(q.v.)* is beginning to wear a bit thin.

Luffness (LUF-nes) *n.*
Hearty feeling that comes from walking on the moors with rubber boots and cold ears.

Lulworth (LUL-wurth) *n.*
(Measure of conversation) A lulworth defines the amount of the length, loudness and embarrassment of a statement you make when everyone else in the room unaccountably stops talking at the same moment.

LUSBY

Luppitt (LUP-pit) *n.*
The piece of leather which hangs off the bottom of your shoe before you can be bothered to get it mended.

Lupridge (LUP-ridj) *n.*
A bubble behind a piece of wallpaper.

Lusby (LUZ-bee) *n.*
The fold of flesh pushing forward over the top of a bra which is too small for the lady inside it.

Luton (LOO-tn) *n.*
The horseshoe-shaped rug which goes around a lavatory seat.

Lutton Gowts (LUT-ton-GOWTS) *n.*
The opposite of green thumbs—the effortless propensity to cause plant death.

Lybster (LIB-ster) *n.*
The artificial chuckle in the voice-over at the end of a supposedly funny television commercial.

Lydd (LID) *n.*
A lid. A lydd differs from a lid in that it has nothing to be a lid of, is at least eighteen months old, and is sold in Ye Olde Antique Shoppes.

Lydiard Tregoze (LID-ee-ard tre-GOHZ) *n.*
The opposite of a mavis enderby *(q.v.)*. An unrequited early love of your life who inexplicably still causes terrible pangs even though she married a telephone engineer.

Lyminster (LIGH-min-ster) *n.*
A homosexual vicar.

Lynwilg (lin-WILG) *n.*
One of those things that pulls the electric cord back into a vacuum cleaner.

Maaruig (Maa-aa-aa-aa-aa-aaaaaaaaaargh-arrrgh-RUOOUOUOU-
ighkh [*]) *n.*
The inexpressible horror experienced on waking up in the morning
and remembering that you are still Scotty in *Star Trek*.

Macroy (ma-KROY) *n.*
An authoritative, confident opinion based on one you read in a
newspaper.

Malaybalay (ma-LAY-ba-lay) *adj.*
All excited at suddenly remembering a wonderful piece of gossip
that you want to pass on to somebody.

Malibu (MAL-i-boo) *n.*
The height by which the top of a wave exceeds the height to which
you have rolled up your trousers.

Manitoba (man-i-TOH-bah) *n.*
A recourtship ritual. The tentative and reluctant touching of
spouses' toes in bed after a row.

Mankinholes (MANK-in-hohlz) *pl. n.*
The small holes in a loaf of bread which give rise to the momen-
tary suspicion that something may have made its home within.

Mapledurham (MAY-pul DUR-um) *n.*
A hideous piece of chipboard veneer furniture bought in a subur-
ban main-street furniture store and designed to hold exactly a
year's supply of Sunday color supplements.

*Loudly, as if in pain.

Margaretting Tye (mah-gah-RET-ing-tigh) *n.*
The unexpectedly intimate bond that forms between two people you introduce to each other, who then exclude you.

Margate (MAHR-gayt) *n.*
A margate is a particular kind of commissionaire who sees you every day and is on cheerful Christian-name terms with you, then one day refuses to let you in because you've forgotten your identity card.

Market Deeping (MAHR-ket-DEE-ping) *ptcpl. vb.*
Stealing a single piece of fruit from a street stall.

Marlow (MAHR-loh) *n.*
The bottom drawer in the kitchen your mother keeps her paper bags in.

Marytavy (MAIR-ee-TAY-vee) *n.*
A person to whom, under dire injunctions of silence, you tell a secret which you wish to be far more widely known.

Masberry (MAS-ber-ee) *n.*
The sap of a giant Nigerian tree from which all cafeteria jams are made.

Massachusetts (MAS-a-CHOO-sets) *pl. n.*
Those items and particles which people who have just blown their noses are searching for when they look into their hankies.

Mavesyn Ridware (MAYV-sin RID-wair) *n.*
The stuff belonging to a mavis enderby *(q.v.)* that keeps turning up in odd corners of your house.

Mavis Enderby (MAY-vis EN-der-bee) *n.*
The almost completely forgotten girlfiend from your distant past for whom your wife has a completely irrational jealousy and hatred.

Maynooth (may-NOOTH) *n.*
> One who recklessly tells total strangers to cheer up, it may never happen.

Meadle (MEE-dul) *vb.*
> To blunder around a woman's breasts in a way that does absolutely nothing for her.

Meath (meeth) *adj.*
> Warm and very slightly clammy. Descriptive of the texture of your hands after you've tried to dry them on a hot-air-blowing automatic hand-drying machine.

Melbury Bubb (MEL-ber-ee BUB) *n.*
> A TV celebrity who rises to fame by being extremely camp.

Melcombe Regis (MEL-kum REE-jis) *n.*
> The name of the style of decoration used in cocktail lounges in mock-Tudor hotels in Los Angeles.

Melton Constable (MEL-tn KUN-stab-ul) *n.*
> A patent antiwrinkle cream which policemen wear to keep themselves looking young.

Memphis (MEM-fis) *n.*
> The little bits of yellow fluff which get trapped in the hinge of the windshield wipers after polishing the car with a new duster.

Memus (MEE-mus) *n.*
> The little trick people use to remind themselves which is left and which is right.

Meuse (MURZ) *n.*
> A period of complete silence on the radio, which means that it must be tuned to NPR.

Millinocket (MIL-in-ok-et) *n.*
> The thing that rattles around inside an aerosol can.

Milwaukee (mil-WAW-kee) *n.*

The melodious whistling, chanting and humming tone of the mil-waukee can be heard whenever a public lavatory is entered. It is the way the occupants of the cubicles have of telling you there's no lock on their door and you can't come in.

Mimbridge (MIM-bridj) *n.*

That which two very boring people have in common which enables you to get away from them.

Minchinhampton (MIN-chin HAMP-tn) *n.*

The expression on a man's face when he has just zipped up his trousers without due care and attention.

Misool (my-SOOL) *n.*

A mixture of toothpaste and saliva in a washbasin.

Moffat (MOF-fut) *n.*

That part of your coat which is designed to be sat on by the person next to you on a bus.

Mogumber (mug-UM-ber) *n.*

One who goes around complaining that he was cleverer ten years ago.

Mointy (MOYN-tee) *n.*

The last little tear before someone cheers up.

Moisie (MOY-zee) *adj.*

The condition of one's face after performing cunnilingus.

Molesby (MOHLZ-bee) *n.*

The kind of family that drives to the beach and then sits in the car with all the windows closed, reading the *TV Guide* and wearing sid-cups *(q.v.)*.

Monks Toft (MONKS-toft) *n.*

The bundle of hair which is left after a monk has been tonsured, which he keeps tied up with a rubber band and uses for chasing ants away.

MALIBU

Morangie (mor-AN-jee) *adj.*
Faintly nervous that a particular post box "won't work" when posting an important letter.

Motspur (MOT-SPER) *n.*
The fourth wheel of a supermarket cart which looks identical to the other three but renders the cart completely uncontrollable.

Mugeary (moo-GHEER-ee) *n.*
(Medical) The substance from which the unpleasant little yellow globules in the corners of a sleepy person's eyes are made.

Multan (mool-TAHN) *n.*
An infidel who stains his face with walnut juice in order to enter Mecca or appear in a sitcom.

Mummelgum (MUM-ul-gum) *n.*
An unwholesome substance that clings to the fingers of successful tomb robbers.

Munderfield (MUN-der-feeld) *n.*
A meadow selected, while driving past, as being ideal for a picnic

which, from a sitting position, turns out to be full of stubble, dust and cowpats and almost impossible to enjoy yourself in.

Munster (MUNS-ter) *n.*
A person who continually brings up the subject of property prices.

Naas (NAHS) *n.*
The wine-making region of Albania where most of the Aasleagh (*q.v.*) comes from.

Nacton (NAK-ton) *n.*
The 'n' with which cheap advertising copywriters replace the word *and* (as in "fish 'n' chips," "mix 'n' match," "assault 'n' battery"), in the mistaken belief that it is in some way chummy or endearing.

Nad (nad) *n.*
Measure defined as the distance between a driver's outstretched fingertips and the ticket machine in an automatic parking lot. One nad = 18.4 cm.

Namber (NAM-ber) *vb.*
To hang around the table being too shy to sit next to the person you really want to.

Nanhoron (nan-HOR-on) *n.*
A tiny valve concealed in the inner ear which enables a deaf grandmother to converse quite normally when she feels like it, but which excludes completely anything which sounds like a request to help with setting the table.

Nantucket (nan-TUK-et) *n.*
   The secret pocket that eats your train ticket.

Nantwich (NANT-wich) *n.*
   A late-night snack, invented by the Earl of Nantwich, which consists of the dampest thing in the fridge. The Earl, who lived in a flat in Clapham, invented the nantwich to avoid having to go shopping.

Naples (NAY-puls) *pl. n.*
   The tiny depressions in a piece of Ryvita.

NAPLES

Naugatuck (NAW-ger-tuk) *n.*
   A plastic packet containing shampoo, mustard, etc., which is impossible to open except by biting off the corners.

Nazeing (NAY-zing) *ptcpl. vb.*
   The rather unconvincing noises of pretended interest which an adult has to make when brought a small dull object for admiration by a child.

Neen Sollars (NEEN SOL-erz) *pl. n.*
Any ensemble of especially unflattering and peculiar garments worn by someone which tells you that they are right at the forefront of fashion.

Nempnett Thrubwell (NEMP-net THRUB-wel) *n.*
The feeling experienced when driving off for the very first time on a brand-new motorbike.

Nindigully (NIN-di GULL-i) *n.*
One who constantly needs to be repersuaded of something they've already agreed to.

Nipishish (ni-PISH-ish) *adj.*
Descriptive of a person walking barefoot on gravel.

Nith (nith) *n.*
The dark piece of velvet which has been brushed against the nap.

Noak Hoak (NOH-kohk) *n.*
A driver who indicates left and turns right.

Nogdam End (NOG-dam-END) *n.*
That part of a pair of scissors used to bang in a picture hook.

Nokomis (noh-KOH-mis) *n.*
One who dresses like an ethnic minority to which they do not belong.

Nome (nohm) *sfx.*
Latin suffix meaning: question expecting the answer "Oh, really? How interesting."

Nossob (NOS-ob) *n.*
Any word that looks as if it's probably another word backwards but turns out not to be.

Nottage (NOT-idj) *n.*
> The collective name for things which you find a use for immediately after you have thrown them away. For instance, your greenhouse has been cluttered up for years with a huge piece of cardboard and great fronds of gardening string. You at last decide to clear all this stuff out, and you burn it. Within twenty-four hours you will urgently need to wrap a large parcel, and suddenly remember that luckily in your greenhouse there is some cardb . . .

Nubbock (NUB-uk) *n.*
> The kind of person who has to leave before a party can relax and enjoy itself.

Nuncargate (nun-KAR-gayt) *adj.*
> Able to go on a two-week holiday with hardly any luggage.

Nundle (NUN-dul) *vb.*
> To move a piano.

Nupend (NEW-pend) *n.*
> The amount of small change found in the lining of an old jacket which just saves your bacon.

Nutbourne (NUT-born) *n.*
> In a choice between two or more possible desserts, the one nobody plumps for.

Nyarling (NYAR-ling) *ptcpl. vb.*
> Of married couples, using a term of endearment as a term of censure or reproach.

Nybster (NIB-ster) *n.*
> The sort of person who takes the elevator to travel one floor.

Ocilla (oh-SILL-er) *n.*
The cute little circle or heart over an *i* used by teenage girls when writing their names.

Ockle (OK-ul) *n.*
An electrical switch which appears to be off in both positions.

Offleyhoo (OF-lee-HOO) *adj.*
Ridiculously overenthusiastic about going to the Pacific Northwest.

Offord Darcy (off-er DAR-see) *n.*
A gate-crasher you can't get rid of because he's become the life and soul of the party.

Old Cassop (OLD KAS-up) *n.*
Piece of caring reassurance which all parties know is completely untrue. As in "a load of . . ."

Ompton (OMP-ton) *n.*
One who has been completely outfitted at Burberry's but is still, nevertheless, clearly from Idaho.

Osbaston (OZ-bas-ton) *n.*
A point made for the seventh time to somebody who insists that he knows exactly what you mean but clearly hasn't got the faintest idea.

Oshkosh (OSH-kosh) *n.*
The noise made by someone who has just been grossly flattered and is trying to make light of it.

Ospringe (OS-prindj) *n.*

That part of a three-color ballpoint which renders it instantly useless.

Ossett (OS-et) *n.*

A frilly spare-toilet-roll cosy.

OSSETT

Ossining (OS-in-ing) *ptcpl. vb.*

Trying to see past the person sitting in front of you in the cinema.

Oswaldtwistle (OS-wald-TWIS-ul) *n.*

(Old Norse) Small brass wind instrument used for summoning Vikings to lunch when they're off on their longships, playing.

Oswestry (OZ-wes-tree) *n.*

The inability to find a comfortable position to lie in bed.

Oughterby (AW-ter-bee) *n.*

Someone you don't want to invite to a party but whom you know you have to as a matter of duty.

Oundle (OWN-dul) *vb.*
To walk along leaning sideways, with one arm hanging limp and dragging one leg behind the other. Most commonly used by actors in amateur productions of *Richard III*, or by people carrying a heavy suitcase in one hand.

Oystermouth (OY-ster-mowth) *n.*
One who can kiss and chew gum at the same time.

Ozark (O-zark) *n.*
One who offers to help just after all the work has been done.

Pabbay (PAB-ay) *n.*
(Fencing term) The play, or maneuver, where one swordsman leaps onto the table and pulls the battle-ax off the wall.

Pant-y-Wacco (PAN-tee WAK-oh) *adj.*
The final state of mind of a retired colonel before they come to take him away.

Pantperthog (pant-PERT-hog) *n.*
An actor whose only talent is to stay fat.

Papcastle (PAP-kah-sul) *n.*
Something drawn or modeled by a small child which you are supposed to know what it is.

Papigochic (PAP-ee-goh-SHEEK) *n.*
A middle-aged man's overlong haircut, intended to make him look younger.

Papple (PAP-ul) *vb.*
To do what babies do to soup with their spoons.

Papworth Everard (PAP-werth EV-er-ard) *n.*
Technical term for the fifth take of an orgasm scene during the making of a pornographic film.

Paradip (PA-ra-dip) *n.*
Polite word for the act of washing one's genitals in the washbasin.

Parbold (PAH-bohld) *adj.*
Nearly brave enough to dive into a cold swimming pool on a windy day.

Parrog (PAR-rog) *n.*
God knows. Could be some sort of bird, I suppose.

Pathstruie (pahth-STROO-ee) *adj.*
The condition of a parish church after a heavy Saturday afternoon's wedlock.

Patkai Bum (PAT-kigh BUM) *n.*
Mysterious illness that afflicts recently deposed heads of state and means they aren't well enough to stand trial.

Patney (PAT-nee) *n.*
Something your next-door neighbor makes and insists that you try on your sausages.

Peebles (PEE-buls) *pl. n.*
Small, carefully rolled pellets of skegness *(q.v.)*.

Peening Quarter (PEE-ning KWAW-ter) *n.*
That area of a discotheque where single men lounge about trying to look groovy about not having the courage to ask a girl to dance.

Pelutho (pel-OOTH-oh) *n.*
A South American ball game. The balls are whacked against a brick wall with a stout wooden bat until the prisoner confesses.

Pen tre-tafarn-y-fedw (PEN TRET-ah FAHN ee FED-oo *) *n.*
Welsh word which literally translates as "leaking-ballpoint-by-
the-glass-hole-of-the-clerk-of-the-bank-has-been-taken-to-
another-place-leaving-only-the-special-inkwell-and-three-inches-
of-tin-chain."

Penge (PENJ) *n.*
The expanding slotted arm on which a cuckoo comes out of a
cuckoo clock.

Peoria (pee-OR-ee-ah) *n.*
The fear of peeling too few potatoes.

Percyhorner (PER-see HAW-ner) *n.*
(English public-school slang) A prefect whose duty it is to sur-
prise new boys at the urinal and humiliate them in a manner of
his choosing.

Perranzabuloe (per-an ZAB-ew-loh) *n.*
One of those spray things used to wet ironing with.

Peru (per-ROO) *n.*
The expression of innocent alarm seen on the face of someone
guiltily surprised in the middle of a perusal.

Peterculter (PEE-ter KUL-ter) *n.*
Someone you don't want to be friends with who rings you up at
eight-monthly intervals and suggests you get together soon.

Pevensey (PEV-en-zee) *n.*
(Archaic) The right to collect shingle from the king's foreshore.

Phillack (FIL-ak) *n.*
A Gucci belt pouch for carrying condoms in.

Pibsbury (PIBZ-ber-ee) *n.*
The little hole in the end of a toothbrush.

* Probably

Picklenash (PIK-ul-nash) *n.*
The detritus found in wineglasses on the morning after a party.

Piddletrenthide (PID-ul TRENT-highd) *n.*
A trouser stain caused by a wimbledon *(q.v.)*. Not to be confused with a botley *(q.v.)*.

Pidney (PID-ni) *n.*
The amount of coffee in the bottom of a jar which doesn't amount to a spoonful.

Pimlico (PIM-li-koh) *n.*
Small odd-shaped piece of plastic or curious metal component found in the bottom of a kitchen rummage drawer when spring cleaning or looking for Scotch tape.

Pimperne (PIM-pern) *n.*
One of those rubber nodules found on the underneath side of a lavatory seat.

PENGE

Pingandy (pin-GAN-dee) *n.*
An extremely neat old person.

Pingaring (PING-a-ring) *n.*
That part of an oven that nobody wants or knows how to turn off.

Pitlochry (pit-LOKH-ree) *n.*
The background gurgling noise heard in fast-food restaurants caused by people trying to get the last bubbles out of the milk-shakes by slurping loudly through their straws.

Pitroddie (pit-ROD-ee) *n.*
A middle- or upper-class person who affects a working-class style of speech.

Pitsligo (pit-SLIGH-goh) *n.*
Part of traditional mating rite. During the first hot day of spring, all the men in the subway start giving up their seats to ladies and strap-hanging. The purpose of pitsligo is to allow them to demonstrate their manhood by displaying the wet patches under their arms.

Pleeley (PLEE-lee) *adj.*
Descriptive of a drunk person's attempts to be endearing.

Plenmeller (plen-MELL-er) *n.*
The nonwaterproof material that raincoats are made out of.

Pleven (PLEV-un) *n.*
One more, or one less, than the number required.

Plumgarths (PLUM-garths) *pl. n.*
The corrugations on the ankles caused by wearing tight socks.

Pluvigner (PLOO-vig-ner) *n.*
The minuscule hole in the side of a ballpoint pen.

Plymouth (PLIM-uth) *vb.*
To relate an amusing story to someone without remembering that it was he who told it to you in the first place.

Plympton (PLIMP-ton) *n.*
The knob on top of a war memorial.

Pocking (POKK-ing) *n.*
The pointless tapping of a cigarette before getting on with the business of smoking it.

Podebrady (POHD-bray-dee) *n.*
The man in dirty white overalls hired to wander whistling around the corridors of a large corporation to make it look as if the management's getting something done.

Pofadder (POF-ad-er) *n.*
A snake that can't be bothered to bite you.

Poffley End (POF-lee-END) *n.*
The green bit of a carrot.

Poges (POH-jez) *pl. n.*
The lumps of dry powder that remain after cooking a packet of soup.

Polbathic (pol-BATH-ik) *adj.*
Gifted with ability to manipulate taps using only the feet.

Pollatomish (pol-i-TOH-mish) *adj.*
Peevish, restless, inclined to pull the stuffing out of sofas.

Polloch (POL-ukh) *n.*
One of those tiny ribbed-plastic and aluminium foil tubs of milk served on trains enabling you to carry one safely back to your compartment where you can spill the contents all over your legs in comfort trying to get the bloody thing open.

Polperro (pol-PER-oh) *n.*
The ball, or muff, of soggy hair found clinging to bath overflow holes.

Polyphant (POL-i-fant) *n.*
> The mythical beast—part bird, part snake, part jam stain—which invariably wins children's painting competitions in the five-to-seven age group.

Pontybodkin (PON-tee-BOD-kin) *n.*
> The stance adopted by a seaside comedian that tells you that the punch line is imminent.

Poona (POO-nah) *n.*
> Satisfied grunting noise made when sitting back after a good meal.

Potarch (POT-ark) *n.*
> The eldest male in a soap opera family.

Pott Shrigley (POT SHRIG-lee) *n.*
> Dried remains of a week-old casserole, eaten when extremely drunk at 2:00 A.M.

Prague (PRAHG) *vb.*
> To declaim loudly and pompously upon any subject about which one has less knowledge than at least one other person at the table.

Preston Gubbals (PRES-ton GUB-uls) *n.*
> Breasts of uneven weight.

Princes Risborough (PRIN-ses RIZ-bur-ah) *n.*
> The right of any member of the Royal Family to have people laugh at their jokes, however weedy.

Prungle (PRUN-gul) *adj.*
> Pretending to be proud to be single.

Pudsey (PUD-zee) *n.*
> The curious-shaped flat wads of dough left on a kitchen table after someone has been cutting out scones.

Pulverbatch (PUL-ver-batch) *n.*

That part of the blurb on a dust jacket in which famous authors claim to have had a series of menial jobs in their youth.

Puning (PEW-ning) *ptcpl. vb.*

Boosting a man's ego by pretending to be unable to open a screw-top jar.

Pymble (PIM-bul) *n.*

Small metal object about the size of a thimble which lies on the ground. When you kick it you discover it is the top of something buried four feet deep.

Quabbs (KWOBZ) *pl. n.*

The substances which emerge when you squeeze a blackhead.

Quall (KWAWL) *vb.*

To speak with the voice of one who requires another to do something for him.

Quedgeley (KWEDJ-lee) *n.*

A rabidly left-wing politician who can afford to be that way because he married a millionairess.

Quenby (KWEN-bee) *n.*

A stubborn spot on a window that you spend twenty minutes trying to clean off before discovering it's on the other side of the glass.

Querrin (KWER-rin) *n.*

A person who no one has ever heard of who unaccountably manages to make a living writing prefaces.

QUABBS

Quoyness (KWOY-nes) *n.*
The hatefulness of words like *relionus* and *KopyKwik*.

Radlett (RAD-let) *n.*
The single hemisphere of dried pea which is invariably found in an otherwise spotlessly clean saucepan.

Ramsgate (RAMZ-gayt) *n.*
All institutional buildings must, by law, contain at least twenty ramsgates. These are doors which open the opposite way to the one you expect.

Randers (RAN-ders) *pl.n.*
People who, for their own obscure reasons, try to sleep with people who have slept with members of the Royal Family.

Ranfurly (ran-FER-lee) *adj.*

Fashion of tying ties so that the long thin end dangles below the short fat end.

RANFURLY

Ravenna (rah-VEN-ah) *n.*

Poetic term for the cleavage in a workman's bottom that peeks above the top of his trousers.

Rhymney (RIM-ni) *n.*

That part of a song lyric which you suddenly discover you've been mishearing for years.

Riber (RIGH-ber) *n.*

The barely soiled sheet of toilet paper that signals the end of the bottom-wiping process.

Richmond (RICH-mnd) *adj.*
Descriptive of the state that very respectable elderly ladies get into if they have a little too much sherry, which, as everyone knows, does not make you drunk.

Rickling (RIK-ling) *ptcpl. vb.*
Fiddling around inside a magazine to remove all the stapled-in special-offer cards that make it impossible to read.

Rigolet (RIG-oh-let) *n.*
As much of an opera as most people can sit through.

Rimbey (RIM-bee) *n.*
The particularly impressive throw of a Frisbee which causes it to be lost.

Ripon (RIP-on) *vb.*
(Of literary critics.) To include all the best jokes from the book in the review to make it look as if the critic thought of them.

Risplith (RIS-plith) *n.*
The burst of applause that greets the sound of a plate smashing in a canteen.

Rochester (RO-ches-ter) *n.*
One who is able to gain occupation of the armrests on both sides of their cinema or aircraft seat.

Roosebeck (RUUS-bek) *n.*
Useful all-purpose emergency word. When a child asks, "Daddy, what's that bird/flower/funny thing that man's wearing?" you simply reply, "It's a roosebeck, darling."

Royston (ROYS-ton) *n.*
The man behind you in church who sings with terrific gusto almost three-quarters of a tone off the note.

Rudge (RUDJ) *n.*
An unjust criticism of your ex-girlfriend's new boyfriend.

Rufforth (RUFF-orth) *n.*
One who has the strength of character or loudness of voice to bring a lowthering *(q.v.)* session to an end.

S

Sadberge (SAD-berdj) *n.*
A violent green shrub which is ground up, mixed with twigs and gelatin and served with clonmult *(q.v.)* and buldoo *(q.v.)* in a container referred to for no known reason as the "relish tray."

Saffron Walden (SAF-ron WAWL-don) *n.*
A particular kind of hideous casual jacket that nobody wears in real life, but which is much favored by Ed McMahon.

Salween (sal-WEEN) *n.*
A faint taste of dishwashing liquid in a cup of tea.

Samalaman (sam-AL-a-man) *n.*
One who fills in the gaps in conversations by beaming genially at people and saying, "Well, well, well, here we all are then," a lot.

Satterthwaite (SAT-er-thwayt) *vb.*
To spray the person you are talking to with half-chewed breadcrumbs or small pieces of whitebait.

Saucillo (saw-SIL-oh) *n.*

A joke told by someone who completely misjudges the temperament of the person to whom it is told.

Savernake (SAV-an-ayk) *v.*

To sew municipal crests onto a jacket in the belief that this will make the wearer appear cosmopolitan.

Scackleton (SKAK-ul-tn) *n.*

Horizontal avalanche of cassettes that slides across the interior of a car as it goes around a sharp corner.

Scamblesby (SKAM-bulz-bee) *n.*

A small dog which resembles a throw rug and appears to be dead.

SCAMBLESBY

Scethrog (SKETH-rog) *n.*

One of those peculiar beards-without-mustaches worn by religious Belgians which help them look like trolls.

Sconser (SKON-ser) *n.*

A person who looks around them when talking to you, to see if there's anyone more interesting about.

Scopwick (SKOP-wik) *n.*

The flap of skin which is torn off your lip when trying to smoke an untipped cigarette.

Scorrier (SKOR-ee-er) *n.*

A small hunting dog trained to snuffle amongst your private parts.

Scosthrop (SKOS-throp) *vb.*

To make vague opening or cutting movements with the hands when wandering about looking for a can opener, scissors, etc., in the hope that this will help in some way.

Scrabby (SKRAB-ee) *n.*

A dustrag given to you by your mother which on closer inspection turns out to be half an underpant.

Scrabster (SKRABZ-ter) *n.*

One of those dogs that has it off on your leg during tea.

Scramoge (skrah-MOHZH) *vb.*

To cut oneself while licking envelopes.

Scranton (SKRAN-ton) *n.*

A person who, after the declaration of the bodmin *(q.v.)*, always says, "But I only had the tomato soup."

Scraptoft (SKRAP-toft) *n.*

The absurd flap of hair a vain and balding man grows long above one ear to comb it plastered over the top of his head to the other ear.

Screeb (SKREEB) *n.*

To make the noise of a nylon windbreaker rubbing against a pair of corduroy trousers.

Screggan (SKREG-en) *n.*

(Banking) The crossed-out bit caused by people putting the wrong year on their checks all through January.

Scremby (SKREM-bee) *n.*
The dehydrated felt-tip pen attached by a string to the "Don't Forget" board in the kitchen, which has never worked in living memory but which no one can be bothered to throw away.

Scridain (skri-DAYN) *n.*
The tone that Gore Vidal adopts with interviewers.

Scroggs (SKROGZ) *n.*
The stout pubic hairs which protrude from your helping of moussaka in a cheap Greek restaurant.

Scronkey (SKRON-kee) *n.*
Something that hits the window as a result of a violent sneeze.

Scugog (SKOO-gog) *n.*
One whose mouth actually hangs open when watching something mildly interesting on the other side of the street.

Scullet (SKUL-et) *n.*
The last teaspoon in the washing up.

Scurlage (SKER-lidj) *n.*
A duck web of snot caused by sneezing into your hand.

Seattle (see-AT-ul) *vb.*
To make a noise like a train going along.

Shalunt (shah-LUNT) *n.*
One who wears Trinidad and Tobago T-shirts on the beach in Bali to prove he didn't just win the holiday in a competition or anything.

Shanklin (SHANK-lin) *n.*
The hoop of skin around a single slice of salami.

Sheepy Magna (SHEEP-ee MAG-nah) *n.*
One who emerges unexpectedly from the wrong bedroom in the morning.

Sheppey (SHEPP-i) *n.*
> Measure of distance (equal to approximately seven-eighths of a mile), defined as the closest distance at which sheep remain picturesque.

Shifnal (SHIF-nal) *n.*
> An awkward shuffling walk caused by two or more people in a hurry accidentally getting in the same segment of a revolving door.

Shimpling (SHIMP-ling) *ptcpl. vb.*
> Lying about the state of your life in order to cheer up your parents.

Shirmers (SHER-merz) *pl. n.*
> Tall young men who stand around smiling at weddings as if to suggest that they know the bride rather well.

Shoeburyness (SHOO-bree-nes) *n.*
> The vague uncomfortable feeling you get when sitting on a seat that is still warm from somebody else's bottom.

Shottle (SHOT-ul) *n.*
> One of those tubes made of yellow plastic that builders use to get rubble off the top floor of a house.

Shrenk (SHRENK) *n.*
> A fold in a pair of stockings that aren't tight enough for a pair of thin legs.

Sicamous (SIK-a-mus) *adj.*
> Perfectly willing to appear on the Jay Leno show.

Sidcup (SID-kup) *n.*
> One of those hats made from tying knots in the corners of a handkerchief.

Sigglesthorne (SIG-ulz-thorn) *n.*
> Anything used in lieu of a toothpick.

Silesia (sigh-LEE-zee-ah) *n.*
(Medical) The inability to remember, at the critical moment, which is the better side of the boat to be seasick off. ·

Silloth (SILL-oth) *n.*
Something that was sticky, and is now furry, found on the carpet under the sofa on the morning after a party.

Simprim (SIM-prim) *n.*
The little movement of false modesty by which a woman with a cavernous visible cleavage pulls her skirt down over her knees.

Sittingbourne (SITT-ing-bawrn) *n.*
One of those conversations where both people are waiting for the other one to shut up so they can get on with their bit.

Skagway (SKAG-way) *n.*
Sudden outbreak of cones strung on a highway.

Skannerup (SKAN-er-oop) *n.*
A Swedish casserole made of elk livers.

Skegness (skeg-NES) *n.*
Nose excreta of a malleable consistency.

Skellister (SKEL-is-ter) *n.*
A very, very old solicitor.

Skellow (SKEL-low) *adj.*
Descriptive of the satisfaction experienced when looking at a really good dry-stone wall.

Skenfrith (SKEN-frith) *n.*
The flakes of athlete's foot found inside socks.

Sketty (SKETT-i) *n.*
Apparently self-propelled little dance a beer glass performs in its own puddle.

Skibbereen (SKIB-er-EEN) *n.*
The noise made by a sunburned thigh leaving a plastic chair.

Skoonspruit (SKOON-sproo-it) *n.*
The tiny garden sprinkler thing your mouth sometimes does for no apparent reason.

Skrubburdnut (SKRUB-urd-nut) *n.*
One who draws penises on posters of women in the subway.

Skulamus (SKUL-a-mus) *n.*
Someone who is obviously not doing what he went into the lavatory for.

Slabberts (SLAB-erts) *pl. n.*
People who say, "Can I have some more juice?" when they mean gravy.

Slettnut (SLET-nut) *n.*
Something that goes round and round but won't come off.

Slipchitsy (SLIP-chit-si) *n.*
Someone who takes the morning off work in order to sign on.

Slobozia (sloh-BOH-zee-ah) *n.*
A chronic inability to pick up underpants.

Slogarie (sloh-GAR-ee) *n.*
Hillwalking dialect for the stretch of concealed rough moorland which lies between what you thought was the top of the hill and what actually is.

Sloinge (SLOYNJ) *n.*
A post-wank tristesse.

Sloothby (SLOOTH-bee) *adj.*
Conspicuously inconspicuous—as of a major celebrity entering a restaurant with a great display of being incognito.

Slubbery (SLUB-er-ee) *n.*

The gooey drips of wax that dribble down the sides of a candle.

Sluggan (SLUG-en) *n.*

A lurid facial bruise that everyone politely omits to mention because it's obvious that you had a punch-up with your spouse last night—but which was actually caused by walking into a door. It is useless to volunteer the true explanation because nobody will believe it.

Slumbay (SLUM-bay) *n.*

The cigarette end someone discovers in the mouthful of lager they have just swigged from a can at the end of a party.

Smarden (SMAR-den) *vb.*

To keep your mouth shut by smiling determinedly through your teeth. Smardening is largely used by people trying to give the impression that they're enjoying a story they've heard at least six times before.

Smearisary (SMEER-is-air-ee) *n.*

The part of a kitchen wall reserved for the schooltime daubings of small children.

Smisby (SMIZ-bee) *n.*

The correct name for a junior apprentice greengrocer whose main duty is to arrange the fruit so that the bad side is underneath. From the name of a character not in Dickens.

Smyrna (SMUR-nah) *n.*

The expression on the face of one whose joke has gone down rather well.

Sneem (SNEEM) *n.*

Particular kind of frozen smile bestowed on a small child by a parent in mixed company when the question "Mummy, what's this?" appears to require the answer, "Er . . . it's a condom, darling."

Snitter (SNIT-er) *n.*
One of the rather unfunny newspaper clippings pinned to an office wall, the humor of which is supposed to derive from the fact that the headline contains a name similar to that of one of the occupants of the office.

Snitterby (SNIT-er-bee) *n.*
Someone who pins up snitters *(q.v.)*.

Snitterfield (SNIT-er-feeld) *n.*
Office bulletin board on which snitters *(q.v.)*, cards saying "You don't have to be crazy to work here, but if you are, it helps!!!" and smutty postcards from Ibiza get pinned up by snitterbies *(q.v.)*.

Snoul (SNOOL) *n.*
The third recurrence of a winter cold.

Snover (SNOH-ver) *n.*
One who is reduced to drinking coffee from his egg-cups in order to put off the dishwashing just one more week.

Solent (SOH-lent) *adj.*
Descriptive of the state of serene self-knowledge reached through drink.

Soller (SOLL-er) *vb.*
To break something in two while testing if you glued it together properly.

Sompting (SOMP-ting) *n.*
The practice of dribbling involuntarily into one's own pillow.

Sotterley (SOTT-er-lee) *n.*
Uncovered bit between two shops with awnings, which you have to cross when it's raining.

Southwick (SOWTH-wik) *n.*
A left-handed wanker.

Spiddle (SPID-ul) *vb.*
To fritter away a perfectly good life pretending to develop film projects.

Spinwam (SPIN-wam) *n.*
The toxic foam that clings to rocky foreshores.

Spittal of Glenshee (SPIT-ul ov glen-SHEE) *n.*
That which has to be cleaned off castle floors in the morning after a bagpipe-playing contest or vampire attack.

Spoffard (SPOF-ard) *n.*
A congressman whose contribution to politics is limited to saying "Hear, hear."

Spofforth (SPOF-orth) *vb.*
To tidy up a room before the cleaning lady arrives.

Spokane (spoh-KANE) *vb.*
To remove precious objects from a room before a party.

Spreakley (SPREEK-lee) *adj.*
Irritatingly cheerful in the morning.

Spruce Knob (SPRUUS NOB) *n.*
A genital aftershave which is supposed to be catching on in the professional tennis circuit.

Spurger (SPUR-jer) *n.*
One who in answer to the question "How are you?" actually tells you.

Spuzzum (SPUZ-um) *n.*
A weewee that resembles a lawn sprinkler, caused by a shred of tissue paper covering the exit hole of the penis.

Squibnocket (SKWIB-nok-et) *n.*
That part of a car, the unexpected need for the replacement of which causes garage bills to be four times larger than the estimate.

Stagno di Gumbi (STAG-noh-dee-GOOM-bee) *n.*
(Italian) Pissed off with waiting for a bus to arrive, a waiter to bring a menu or a genius to finish painting your ceiling.

Staplow (STAP-loh) *n.*
A telephone number that you now can't find anywhere because two years ago you swore you would never speak to the person again.

Stebbing (STEB-ing) *n.*
The erection you cannot conceal because you are not wearing a jacket.

Steenhuffel (STEEN-huf-ul) *n.*
One who is employed by a trade delegation or negotiating team to swell the numbers and make it look impressive when they walk out. There are currently 25,368 steenhuffels working at the UN in New York.

Stelling Minnis (STEL-ing MIN-is) *n.*
A traditional street dance. This lovely old gigue can be seen at any time of the year in the streets of the City of London or the courts of the Old Bailey. Wherever you see otherwise perfectly staid groups of bankers, barristers or ordinary members of the public moving along in a slightly syncopated way, you may be sure that a stelling minnis is taking place. The phenomenon is caused by the fact that the dancers are trying not to step on the cracks in the pavement in case the bears get them.

Stibb (STIB) *n.*
An unwelcome poke in the ribs by someone who hardly knows you.
"Mr Robert Maxwell stibbed Her Royal Highness repeatedly with his huby *(q.v.)*."
—The *Times*

Stibbard (STIB-ard) *n.*
The invisible brake pedal on the passenger's side of the car.

Stody (STOH-dee) *n.*
The small drink that someone nurses for hours so they can stay in the pub.

Stoke Poges (STOHK POH-jiz) *n.*
The tapping movements of an index finger on glass made by a person futilely attempting to communicate with either a tropical fish or a post office clerk.

Stowting (STOWT-ing) *ptcpl. vb.*
Feeling a pregnant woman's tummy.

Strassgang (STRAHS-gang) *n.*
German word for the group of workers hired to lunch inside a string of highway cones, or skagway *(q.v.)*.

Strelley (STREL-ee) *n.*
Long strip of paper or tape that has got tangled around the wheel of something.

Strubby (STRUB-i) *adj.*
Attractively miniature.

Sturry (STUH-ri) *n.*
A token run. Pedestrians who have chosen to cross a road immediately in front of an approaching vehicle generally give a little wave and break into a sturry. This gives the impression of hurrying without having any practical effect on their speed whatsoever.

Stutton (STUT-on) *n.*
Tiny melted plastic nodule which fails to help fasten a duvet cover.

Suckley Knowl (SUK-lee-nohl) *n.*
A plumber's assistant who never knows where the actual plumber is.

Surby (SER-bee) *adj.*
Insolently polite, as of policemen who have stopped a motorist.

Sutton and Cheam (SUT-un-and-CHEEM) *Nouns*
Sutton and cheam are the two kinds of dirt into which all dirt is divided. "Sutton" is the dark sort that always gets onto light-colored things, and "cheam" the light-colored sort that always clings onto dark items. Anyone who has ever found peanut butter stains on a dress-shirt, or sea gull goo on a tuxedo, (a) knows all about sutton and cheam, and (b) is going to some very curious dinner parties.

Swaffham Bulbeck (SWAF-um BUL-bek) *n.*
An entire picnic lunch spent fighting off wasps.

Swanage (SWON-idj) *pl. n.*
A series of diversionary tactics used when trying to cover up the existence of a glossop *(q.v.)*, such as uttering a high-pitched laugh and pointing out of the window.

Swanibost (SWON-i-bost) *adj.*
Completely shagged out after a hard day having income tax explained to you.

Swefling (SWEF-ling) *ptcpl.vb*
Using a special attachment to vacuum a sofa.

Symond's Yat (SIGH-mondz YAT) *n.*
The little spoonful inside the lid of a recently opened boiled egg.

T

Tabley Superior (TAB-lee soo-PEER-ee-er) *n.*
The look directed at you in a theater bar during the interval by people who've already got their drinks.

Tampa (TAM-pah) *n.*
The sound of a rubber eraser coming to rest after dropping off a desk in a very quiet room.

Tananarive (TAN-an-ar-ighv) *vb.*
To announce your entrance by falling over the trash can in the drive.

Tanvats (TAN-vats) *pl. n.*
Disturbing things that the previous owners of your house have left in the cellar.

Tarabulus (ta-RAB-ew-lus) *n.*
The geometrical figure which describes the "Ban the Bomb" sign or a car steering wheel.

Taroom (ta-ROOM) *vb.*
To make loud noises during the night to let the burglars know you are in.

Teigngrace (TAYN-grays) *n.*
The belief that a Devon cream tea is not going to make you feel sick after you've eaten it.

Tew (TEW) *n.*
The tuft of hair that grows between a man's eyebrows.

Tewel (TEW-ul) *n.*
The little brass latch that fastens the front wall of a doll's house.

Throcking (THROK-ing) *ptcpl. vb.*
The action of continually pushing down the lever on a pop-up toaster in the hope that you will thereby get it to understand that you want it to toast something.

Throckmorton (throk-MOR-ton) *n.*
The soul of a departed madman: one of those now known to inhabit the timing mechanisms of pop-up toasters.

Thrumster (THRUM-ster) *n.*

The irritating man next to you at a concert who thinks he's the conductor.

Thrupp (THRUP) *vb.*

To hold a ruler on one end of a desk and make the other end go *bbddbbddbbrrbrrrrddrr.*

Thurnby (THERN-bee) *n.*

A rucked-up edge of carpet or linoleum that everyone says someone will trip over and break a leg unless it gets fixed. After a year or two someone trips over it and breaks a leg.

Tibshelf (TIB-shelf) *n.*

Criss-cross wooden construction hung on a wall in a teenage girl's bedroom, which is covered with glass Bambis and poodles, matching pigs and porcelain ponies in various postures.

Tidpit (TID-pit) *n.*

The corner of a toenail from which satisfying little black spots may be sprung.

Tillicoultry (TIL-ee-KOOL-tree) *n.*

The man-to-man chumminess adopted by an employer as a prelude to telling an employee that he's going to have to let him go.

Timble (TIM-bul) *vb.*

(Of small nasty children) To fall over very gently, look around to see who's about and then yell blue murder.

Tincleton (TINK-ul-tn) *n.*

A man who amuses himself in your lavatory by pulling the chain in mid-pee and then seeing if he can finish before the flush does.

Tingewick (TINJ-wik) *n.*

The first, sleepy morning stirrings of the penis.

Tingrith (TIN-grith) *n.*

The feeling of silver paper against your fillings.

Tockholes (TOK-hohlz) *pl.n.*
The tiny meaningless perforations which infest brogues.

Todber (TOD-ber) *n.*
One whose idea of a good time is to stand behind his front hedge and give surly nods to people he doesn't know.

Todding (TODD-ing) *vb.*
The business of talking amicably and aimlessly to your local bartender.

Tolob (TOL-ob) *n.*
A crease or fold in an underblanket, the removal of which involves getting out of bed and largely remaking it.

Tolstachaolais (TOL-stakh-ah-ow-ligh-EES *) *phr.*
What the police in Leith require you to say in order to prove that you are not drunk.

Tomatin (TOM-a-tin) *n.*
The chemical from which canned tomato soup is made.

Tonypandy (TOH-nee-PAN-dee) *n.*
The voice used by presenters on children's television programs.

Toodyay (tood-YAY) *n.*
Indonesian expression meaning "some time next month."

Tooting Bec (TOOT-ing-BEK) *n.*
A car behind which one draws up at the traffic lights and honks at when the lights go green before realizing that the car is parked and there is no one inside.

Torlundy (tor-LUN-dee) *n.*
Narrow but thickly grimed strip of floor between the fridge and the sink unit in the kitchen of a rented apartment.

---

* Or just gargle.

Toronto (to-RON-toh) *n.*
Generic term for anything which comes out in a gush despite all your careful efforts to let it out gently, *e.g.,* flour into a white sauce, tomato ketchup onto fried fish, sperm into a human being, etc.

Totteridge (TOT-er-idj) *n.*
The ridiculous two-inch hunch that people adopt when arriving late for the theater in the vain hope that it will minimize either the embarrassment or the lack of visibility for the rest of the audience.

Trantlemore (TRANT-ul-mor) *vb.*
To make a noise like a train crossing a set of points.

Trewoofe (tre-WOOF) *n.*
A very thick and heavy drift of snow balanced precariously on the edge of a door porch, waiting for what it judges to be the correct moment to fall. From the ancient Greek legend "The Trewoofe of Damocles."

Trispen (TRIS-pen) *n.*
A form of intelligent grass. It grows a single, tough stalk and makes its home on lawns. When it sees the lawnmower coming it lies down and pops up again after it has gone by.

Trossachs (TROSS-akhs) *pl. n.*
The useless epaulettes on an expensive raincoat.

Trunch (TRUNCH) *n.*
Instinctive resentment of people younger than you.

Tuamgraney (TOO-am GRAY-nee) *n.*
A hideous wooden ornament that people hang over the mantelpiece to prove they've been to Africa.

Tukituki (TOO-kee TOO-kee) *n.*
A sexual liaison that is meant to be secret but that is in fact common knowledge.

Tullynessle (TULL-i-nes-ul) *n.*
An honest attempt to track down a clitoris.

TUAMGRANEY

Tulsa (TUL-sah) *n.*
A slurp of beer that has accidentally gone down your shirt collar.

Tumby (TUM-bee) *n.*
The involuntary abdominal gurgling which fills the silence following someone else's intimate personal revelation.

Tweedsmuir (TWEEDZ-mewr) *collective n.*
The name given to the extensive collection of hats kept in the downstairs lavatory which don't fit anyone in the family.

Twomileborris (TOO-mighl BOR-is) *n.*
A popular East European outdoor game in which the first person to reach the front of the meat queue wins, and the losers have to forfeit their bath plugs.

U

Udine (YEW-dine) *adj.*
 Not susceptible to charm.

Ugglebarnby (UG-ul BARN-bee) *n.*
 The ponytail affected by a middle-aged balding man.

Ullapool (UL-a-pool) *n.*
 The spittle that builds up on the floor of the orchestra pit of the Metropolitan Opera House.

Ullingswick (UL-ing-zwik) *n.*
 An overdeveloped epiglottis found in middle-aged coloraturas.

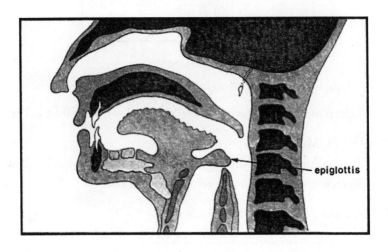

ULLINGSWICK

Ulting (UL-ting) *ptcpl. vb.*
 Clicking the jaw to unpop the ears.

Umberleigh (UM-ber-lee) *n.*
 The awful moment that follows a dorchester *(q.v.)* when a

speaker weighs whether to repeat an amusing remark after nobody laughed the last time. To be "on the horns of an umberleigh" is to wonder whether people didn't hear the remark, or whether they did hear it and just didn't think it was funny,
which was why somebody coughed.

Upottery (up-OTT-er-ee) *n.*
That part of a kitchen cupboard that contains an unnecessarily large number of milk jugs.

Urchfont (ERCH-font) *n.*
Sudden stab of hypocrisy that goes through the mind when taking vows as a godparent.

Uttoxeter (yew-TOK-sit-er) *n.*
A small but immensely complex mechanical device that is essentially the "brain" of a modern coffee machine, and that enables the machine to make its own decisions.

Valletta (va-LET-er) *n.*
An ornate headdress or loose garment worn by a person in the belief that it renders him invisibly native and not like a tourist at all. People who don huge conical straw coolie hats with "I luv Lagos" on them in Nigeria, or fat solicitors on holiday in Malaya who insist on appearing in the hotel lobby wearing a sarong, know what we are talking about.

Vancouver (van-KOO-ver) *n.*
The technical name for one of those huge trucks with whirling brushes on the bottom used to clean streets.

Ventnor (VENT-ner) *n.*

One who, having been visited as a child by a mysterious gypsy lady, is gifted with the strange power of being able to operate the air nozzles above airplane seats.

Vidlin (VID-lin) *n.*

The moistly frayed end of a piece of cotton thread. "It is easier for a rich man to enter the Kingdom of Heaven than it is for a vidlin to pass through the eye of a needle."

VIDLIN

Visby (VIZ-bee) *n.*

The pointy, tentlike structure in the bedclothes with which a man indicates to his partner that he thinks it's high time she stopped fiddling around in the bathroom cupboard and came to bed.

Vollenhove (VOL-un-hohv) *n.*

One who indicates from thirty yards across a crowded street that he has spotted you, wishes to speak with you and that you are required to remain rooted to the spot waiting for him.

Waccamaw (WAK-a-mawr) *n.*
An exotic Brazilian bird which makes its home in the audiences of BBC Light Entertainment Radio shows and screeches when it hears the word "bottom."

Warleggan (waw-LEG-un) *n.*
(Archaic) One who does not approve of araglins *(q.v.)*.

Wartnaby (WAWT-nay-bee) *n.*
Something you only discover about somebody the first time they take their clothes off in front of you.

Wasp Green (WASP GREEN) *adj.*
The paint in the catalog that is quite obviously yellow.

Watendlath (WAT-end-lath) *n.*
The bit of wood a cabbie removes so as to open his sliding window and give you the full benefit of his opinions.

Wawne (WAWN) *n.*
A badly supressed yawn.

Wedderlairs (WED-el-ayrz) *pl. n.*
The large patches of sweat on the back of a hot man's T-shirt.

Wembley (WEM-blee) *n.*
The hideous moment of confirmation that the disaster presaged in the ely *(q.v.)* has actually struck.

Wendens Ambo (WEN-denz AM-boh) *n.*
(Veterinary term) The operation to trace an object swallowed by a cow through all its seven stomachs. Hence, also, an expedition to find the new terminal at O'Hare Airport.

West Wittering (west WIT-er-ing) *ptcpl. vb.*
The uncontrollable twitching that breaks out when you're trying to get away from the most boring person at a party.

Wetwang (WET-wang) *n.*
A moist penis.

Whaplode Drove (WHAP-lohd DROVE) *n.*
A homicidal golf stroke.

Whasset (WHAS-it) *n.*
A business card in your wallet belonging to someone whom you have no recollection of meeting.

Whissendine (WHIS-en-dine) *n.*
A noise that occurs (often at night) in a strange house, which is too short and too irregular for you ever to be able to find out what it is and where it comes from.

Widdicombe (WID-i-kum) *n.*
The sort of person who impersonates telephones.

Wigan (WIG-un) *n.*
If, when talking to someone you know has only one leg, you're trying to treat them perfectly casually and normally, but find to your horror that your conversation is liberally studded with references to (a) Long John Silver, (b) Hopalong Cassidy, (c) the Hokey Pokey, (d) "putting your foot in it," (e) "the last leg of the UEFA competion," you are said to have committed a wigan.

Wike (WIGHK) *vb.*
To rip a Band-Aid off your skin as fast as possible in the hope that it will (a) show how brave you are and (b) not hurt.

Willimantic (WIL-i-MAN-tik) *adj.*
Of a person whose heart is in the wrong place (*i.e.*, between his legs).

Wimbledon (WIM-bul-dun) *n.*

The last drop that, no matter how much you shake it, always goes down your trouser leg.

Winkley (WINK-lee) *n.*

A lost object which turns up immediately after you've gone and bought a replacement for it.

Winster (WIN-ster) *n.*

One who is mistakenly under the impression that he is charming.

Winston-Salem (WIN-ston SAY-lem) *n.*

A person in a restaurant who suggests to his companions that they should split the cost of the meal equally, and then orders two packs of cigarettes on the bill.

WEDDERLAIRS

Wivenhoe (WIV-en-hoh) *n.*

The cry of alacrity with which a sprightly eighty-year-old breaks the ice on the lake when going for a swim on Christmas Eve.

Woking (WOH-king) *ptcpl. vb.*
Standing in the kitchen wondering what you came in here for.

Wollondilly (WOL-un-DIL-ee) *n.*
A woman who can't get her lipstick on straight.

Worgret (WUR-gret) *n.*
A kind of poltergeist that specializes in stealing new road atlases from your car.

Worksop (WURK-sop) *n.*
A person who never actually gets around to doing anything because he spends all his time writing out lists headed "Things to Do (Urgent)."

Wormelow Tump (WUR-ma-loh TUMP) *n.*
Any seventeen-year-old who doesn't know about anything at all in the world other than bicycle gears.

Wrabness (RAB-nes) *n.*
The feeling after having tried to dry oneself with a damp towel.

Writtle (RIT-ul) *vb.*
Of a steel ball, to settle into a hole.

Wroot (ROOT) *n.*
A short little berk who thinks that by pulling on his pipe and gazing shrewdly at you he will give the impression that he is infinitely wise and six feet, two inches tall.

Wubin (WOO-bin) *n.*
The metal foil container which Chinese meals come in.

Wyoming (wigh-OH-ming) *ptcpl. vb.*
Moving in hurried desperation from one cubicle to another in a public lavatory trying to find one that has a lock on the door, a seat on the bowl and no brown streaks on the seat.

Yalardy (ya-LAR-dee) *n.*

An illness which you know you've got but which the thermometer refuses to acknowledge.

Yarmouth (YAR-muth) *vb.*

To shout at foreigners in the belief that the louder you speak, the better they'll understand you.

Yate (YAYT) *n.*

Dishearteningly white piece of bread that sits limply in a pop-up toaster during a protracted throcking *(q.v.)* session.

Yebra (YEE-brah) *n.*

A cross between a zebra and anything else which fancies zebras.

YEBRA

Yesnaby (YES-nay-bee) *n.*

A "yes, maybe" which means "no."

Yetman (YET-man) *n.*

A yes-man who is waiting to see whom it would be most advantageous to agree with.

Yonder Bognie (YON-der-BOG-nee) *n.*

The kind of restaurant advertised as "just three minutes from this cinema" which clearly nobody ever goes to and, even if they had ever contemplated it, have certainly changed their mind since seeing the ad.

Yonkers (YON-kerz) *n.*

(Rare) The combined thrill of pain and shame when being caught in public plucking your nostril hairs and stuffing them into your side pocket.

York (YAWK) *vb.*

To shift the position of the shoulder straps on a heavy bag or rucksack in a vain attempt to make it seem lighter. Hence: to laugh falsely and heartily at an unfunny remark.

"Jasmine yorked politely, loathing him to the depths of her being."

—Virginia Woolf

Z

Zafrilla (za-FRIL-ah) *n.*

A garment that even Zsa Zsa Gabor would not deign to wear.

Zagreb (za-GREB) *n.*

A stranger who suddenly clutches an intimate part of your body and then pretends he did it to prevent himself from falling.

Zeal Monachorum (ZEEL mon-a-KOR-um) *n.*

(Skiing term) To ski with "zeal monachorum" is to descend the top three-quarters of the mountain in a quivering blue funk, but on arriving at the gentle bit just in front of the restaurant to whizz to a stop like a victorious slalom champion.

ZIGONG

Zeerust (ZEE-rust) *n.*

The particular kind of datedness which afflicts things that were originally designed to look futuristic.

Zigong (ZEE-gong) *n.*

Screeching skid made by cartoon character prior to turning around and running back in the opposite direction.

Zlatibor (ZLAT-i-bawr) *n.*

(Hungarian) A prince of the blood royal temporarily forced to seek employment as a waiter.

Zod (ZOD) *n.*

An irritating lump which sticks out from the main body. Hence:

1. A bit of cement which sits proud of the brickwork.

2. A drip of paint on the windowpane.

3. The knob of surplus butter on a corner of toast.

4. Geraldo Rivera's head.

Zumbo (ZUM-boh) *n.*

One who pretends not to know that the muffler has fallen off his car.

iNdEx of MeaNinGs

A

abuse
    scissor: *Nogdam End*
    self, post: *Sloinge*
    self, sinister: *Southwick*

acquaintances
    remote: *Ardcrony*
    who should be more remote:
        Corfu

acronyms, uselessness of: Cafu

actors
    dreadful, amateur: *Aberbeeg*
    dreadful, amateur, lopsided:
        Oundle
    dreadful, fruity: *Hordle*
    dreadful, obese: *Pantperthog*
    dreadful, Scottish, cravat-
        wearing: *Glenduckie*
    dreadful, Shakespearian:
        Damnaglaur
    dreadful, stained: *Multan*

Adair, Red: *Esher*

afternoon
    four o'clock in the: *Brymbo,*
        Farnham
    wasted in front of the
        television: *Gonnabarn*

airports
    behavior of luggage in: *Adlestrop*
    cursed: *Aird of Sleat*

alarms
    burglar: *Framlingham*
    false: *Godalming*
    silent: *Duleek*
    untimely: *Lostwithiel*

Albania, unpleasant beverages of:
    Naas

algae, trouser: *Huttoft*

Americans
    brain-dead: *Lackawanna*
    who aren't fooling anybody:
        Ompton

amounts
    contentious: *Bodmin*
    footling: *Kibblesworth*
    piddling: *Le Touquet*

anatomy
    alarming discoveries about
        someone's: *Wartnaby*
    close proximity between bits
        of: *Moisie*
    confusion between bits of:
        Willimantic
    corrugations on bits of:
        Plumgarths, Des Moines
    horrible bits of: *Aigburth*
    huge dangly strands of:
        Ullingswick
    hunts for bits of: *Tullynessle*
    lovers who are keen on bits
        of your: *Lublin*
    odd connections between
        bits of: *Acklins*
    strangers who are keen on
        bits of your: *Zagreb*
    sweaty bits of: *Elsrickle,*
        Pitsligo
    too frequently honored
        parts of: *Dubbo*
    unwelcome bits of somebody
        else's: *Stibb*
    useless bits of: *Brecon, Clun*
    wide-open bits of: *Scugog*

animals
    attempts to communicate
        with Post Office clerks
        or: *Stoke Poges*
    casual cross-breeding of: *Yebra*

disgusting bits of: *Gruids*
disinclination to be bothered
    to identify: *Parrog, Roosebeck*
doo-doos of (china): *Barstibley*
doo-doos of (metaphorical):
    Euphrates, Old Cassop
doo-doos of (real): *Dogdyke,
    Joliette, Bromsgrove*
eviscerated, Swedish:
    Skannerup
fried: *Toronto*
haughty: *Pofadder*
    mythical, or at least
    unrecognizable: *Polyphant*
things that are like bits of:
    Scurlage
with absurd numbers of
    stomachs: *Wendens Ambo*

ankles
bits above your: *Bogue*
corrugated: *Plumgarths*

answers
deflected: *Ainderby Steeple*
expected: *Nome*
required, embarrassing: *Sneem*
the phone, confusion caused
    when someone: *Gammersgill*
the phone, suspicion caused
    when someone: *Kurdistan*
unwelcome, interminable:
    Spurger

antiques
telephonic: *Aldclune*
useless, definitely fake:
    Brumby
useless, possibly fake: *Lydd*

ants, means of chasing: *Monks Toft*

apologies
loud, interminable: *Hickling*
recursive: *Greeley*
uttered while hopping: *Droitwich*

applause
calculated to generate: *Firebag*

for injury: *Hoddlesdon*
ironic, in cafeteria: *Risplith*

archdeacons, protruberances on the
    noses of: *Botolphs*

arguments
after meals: *Bodmin*
after parties: *Heanton
    Punchardon*
badly planned: *Eakring*
before meals: *Lowther*
chilly consequences of:
    Famagusta
imperceptibly reversed: *Glenties*
manifestly blithering: *Inverinate*
uncharacteristically pertinent:
    Gress

armholes
difficulties with: *Hessle*
excessive number of: *Jurby*

armrests, double helping of: *Rochester*

arms
expanding: *Penge*
limp: *Oundle*
sweat under: *Pitsligo*

aromas
domestic, unwelcome: *Keele*
hirable, unwelcome: *Duluth*
rural, welcome: *Hull*
urban, unwelcome: *Chicago*
urban, welcome: *Lindisfarne*
zoological, romantic: *Dunbar*

around
but don't come off, things that
    go: *Slettnut*
but shouldn't, things that go:
    Strelley
things that don't go: *Adrigole,
    Motspur*
things that go: *Hextable*

arts
ancient, Eastern: *Kalami*
ancient: *Alltami*
domestic, sculptural: *Hepple*

ashtrays
    things used as: *Slumbay*
    washing of: *Keele*

asleep
    bits of you that are: *Clun*
    bits of you that aren't any
        more: *Tingewick*
    things collected while:
        Ambatolampy
    things heard while: *Balzan,
        Bonkle*

assistants
    exorcists' clutching:
        Clenchwarton
    ignorant plumbers': *Suckley
        Knowl*
    ignorant shop: *Hotagen*

attachment
    to a face: *Kirby*
    to a Hoover: *Swefling*
    to a nose: *Botolphs*
    to a string: *Scremby*

attacks
    spasmodic: *Jawcraig*
    vampire: *Spittal of Glenshee*

attempts
    kindly, misguided: *Kirby
        Misperton*
    lecherous, resolute: *Tullynessle*
    lecherous, unsuccessful:
        Farrancassidy
    to see the film you've paid
        good money to watch:
        Ossining

awnings, gushing: *Sotterley*

B

babies
    muckiness of: *Papple*
    stickiness of: *Halcro*
    second thoughts about the
        names of: *Abert*

backs
    of armchairs: *Hassop*
    of cupboards: *Cong*
    of people who are not your
        friends: *Boothby Graffoe*
    of T-shirts: *Wedderlairs*
    of taxis: Low *Ardwello*
    of throats: *Gulberwick*
    things dropped down: *Burton
        Coggles*

backslapping: *Boothby Graffoe*

Bader, Sir Douglas: *Ludlow*

bafflement, nuptials marked by:
    Cowcaddens

bags
    carrier, growing: *Dungeness*
    elderly, deaf: *Nanhoron*
    fearsome, hideous:
        Baughurst
    mulch kept in the bottom of:
        Glud
    paper, maternal: *Marlow*
    slippery, translucent: *Flimby*
    solitary, Scottish:
        Glentaggart

bakers
    least appealing products of:
        Brymbo
    people who show off to:
        Bradworthy

baldness
    graceless reactions to growing:
        Ugglebarnby
    useless attempts to conceal:
        Scraptoft

ballads, raucous old: *Banteer*

ballpoint pens
    holes in: *Pluvigner*
    leaky: *Pen tre-tafarn-y-fedw*
    reason for uselessness of three-
        colored: *Ospringe*
    tied together, six, uselessness
        of: *Ipplepen*

balls
> dangerously odd number of:
> > *Belding*
> soggy, hairy: *Polperro*
> steel, rattling: *Writtle*

Band-Aid, torn off skin: *Wike*

bands, rubber: *Monks Toft*

banks
> rising young managers of:
> > *Hobarris*
> things that confuse: *Albuquerque,*
> > *Screggan*
> Welsh: *Pen tre-tafarn-y-fedw*

bartenders
> aimless: *Todding*
> apparently blind: *Epping*
> surly: *Goole*

barristers
> dancing: *Stelling Minnis*
> greasy: *Glazeley*

bars
> complete berks in: *Louth*
> sandwich: *Darenth*
> theater: *Tabley Superior*
> wet: *Listowel, Goole*

basins
> things found in: Misool,
> > *Hathersage*
> things washed in: *Paradip*

bastards
> bloody rude: *Fovant*
> in technical sense: *Gastard*
> inconsiderate, stupid, filthy:
> > *Dogdyke*
> lazy: *Abinger, Ozark*
> mad and/or lazy: *Bozeman*
> scatty: *Abligo*
> six-year-old: *Little Urswick*
> smooth, beery: *Louth*
> smooth, lecherous, young:
> > *Shirmers*
> smug, shitty, Masonic:
> > *Grimsby*
> vile, vain, rich: *Shalunt*

bathrooms
> attempts to lure people out
> > of: *Visby*
> nocturnal attempts to find:
> > *Islesteps*

baths
> bubbly noises in: *Budle*
> prunelike objects in: *Dewlish*
> round, rubbery objects in:
> > *Dillytop*
> soggy things in: *Polperro*
> turbulent convection in: *Harlosh*

bats
> hairy, harmless old: *Lossiemouth*
> incompetent, well-meaning
> > old: *Jurby*
> stout, wooden: *Pelutho*
> vampire: *Spittal of Glenshee*

battle-axes, sharp, on castlewall:
> *Pabbay*

bddbbrrddbddrr, things that go:
> *Thrupp*

beating: *Aboyne*

bed
> areas to be avoided in:
> > *Hobbs Cross*
> banana-shaped objects on:
> > *Baumber*
> comforting preparations for:
> > *Lambarene*
> dreadful mistakes in: *Hagnaby*
> tent-shaped objects in: *Visby*
> things found in: *Ballycumber*
> things that bounce on:
> > *Abwong, Dunster*
> things that don't work in:
> > *Stutton*
> things that go wrong in:
> > *Brecon*
> things that jump out of:
> > *Duleek*
> thrashing around in:
> > *Oswestry*
> unwelcome lumps in: *Tolob*

bedrooms
    chilly winds in: *Famagusta*
    embarrassing things in hotel:
        Bedfont
    emerging from wrong:
        Sheepy Magna
    guests in spare: *Dunster*
    views into other people's:
        Beaulieu Hill
    young girls': *Tibshelf*

behavior
    facetious, misguided: *Dockery*
    lip: *Gallipoli*
    naughty: *Sheepy Magna*
    nerdlike: *Scugog*
    perverse, sticky: *Ardslignish*

behind
    cleavage in: *Ravenna*
    dragging one leg: *Oundle*
    droplets on: *Elsrickle*
    leaving one's hat: *Hidcote Bartram*

Belgians, hairy, religious: *Scethrog*

beliefs
    creamy, mistaken: *Teignmouth*
    fatuous, entertained abroad:
        Valletta, Yarmouth
    mistaken, humorous: *Dockery*

berks
    check-jacketed, beery: *Louth*
    deliberately forgetful: *Abligo*
    in restaurants: *Ardentinny*
    irritatingly conversational:
        Dalmilling,
    lazy: *Nybster*
    short, pipe-smoking: *Wroot*
    unwanted: *Nubbock*
    who can't tell jokes without
        making a complete hash
        of it: *Jofane*

bicycle gears: *Wormelow Tump*

bills
    anomalous: *Bodmin*
    heart-stopping: *Squibnocket*
    sneakily inflated: *Winston-Salem*

bird
    Brazilian, easily amused:
        Waccamaw
    possible congruence with
        type of: *Parrog*
    sort of half-: *Polyphant*
    unidentifiable: *Roosebeck*

biscuits
    digestive, religious: *Corstorphine*
    fresh, or so they claim:
        Dorridge

bites
    snakes which can't be bothered
        to administer: *Pofadder*
    spots which could be: *Bauple*

bliss
    conjugal, absence of at dinner:
        Balemartine, Inigonish
    conjugal, absence of in bed:
        Famagusta
    conjugal, absence of in car:
        Heanton Punchardon
    conjugal, conducted on
        cheap floormatting: *Bures*
    conjugal, first steps back
        toward: *Manitoba*
    conjugal, invitation to: *Visby*
    conjugal, possible threats to:
        Kurdistan
    conjugal, recurrent threats to:
        Mavis Enderby
    of a really good widdle:
        Gilling

blobs
    bloody-minded: *Glossop*
    dried: *Klosters*
    stubborn: *Quenby*

blowouts, oral: *Berkhamsted*

blue funk: *Zeal Monachorum*

blue murder: *Timble*

boards, don't forget: *Scremby*

book reviews: *Ripon*

books

codswallop written in:
Pulverbatch
fat, expensive: *Great Tosson*
futile attempts to read:
Dalmilling
incomprehensible paragraphs
in: *Fritham*
lavatorial: *Great Wakering*
of matches, not worth
stealing: *Fremantle*
triumphantly finished: *Beppu*
you haven't finished:
Ballycumber
you haven't read at all: *Bathel*

bookshelves: *Ahenny*

bores

low tolerance of: *Lolland*
pompous, any age: *Ardcrony*
principal habitat of: *Burslem*
things induced by: *Wawne*
worst, at a party: *West Wittering*

bottle parties: *Naas, Aasleagh*

bottles

blue: *Bursledon*
gin: *Le Touquet*
ketchup: *Cromarty*
whiskey: *Brumby*

bottom

chill wind that afflicts:
Famagusta
cleavage in workman's: *Ravenna*
exposed: *Grinstead*
huge whirling brushes on:
Vancouver
interesting patterns on own:
Kettering
lip: *Gallipoli*
moist rivulets between the
cheeks of: *Elsrickle*
newly cleaned: *Riber*
of drawers, things found in:
Pimlico
of shoes: *Luppitt*

reaction of Brazilian bird to
mention of: *Waccamaw*
warmth of someone else's:
Shoeburyness

boxes

things upside down in:
Bolsover
in garages: *Kentucky*

boys

high-pitched: *Caarnduncan*
new: *Percyhorner*
with stupid names: *Cheb*

brain

inoperative: *Duntish*
of coffee machine: *Uttoxeter*

bras

impossible: *Farrancassidy*
inadequate: *Lusby*

bread

airborne crumbs of: *Satterthwaite*
hundred slices of: *Darenth*
single slice of: *Yate*
wildlife in: *Mankinholes*

break

a leg: *Thurnby*
into something that clearly
isn't a run: *Sturry*
something you've just glued
together: *Soller*
the ice: *Wivenhoe*
up, are they going to?:
Badachonacher

breasts

attempted access to:
Farrancassidy
clumsy business with: *Meadle*
lopsided: Preston *Gubbals*
only semicontained: *Lusby*

breath

condensation of: *Brithdir*
extruded through noses:
Burbage

breezes, in armpit: *Kimmeridge*

bristles: *Aith*

Bronson, Charles: *Duncraggon*

bruises
  honorably acquired: *Dubbo*
  virulent, accidental: *Sluggan*
  yellowing, inexplicable: *Ampus*

bubbles
  behind wallpaper: *Lupridge*
  congealed, cheesy: *Eriboll*
  flatulent: *Budle*
  slurped, milky: *Pitlochry*

buffers
  boring, old: *Ainderby Quernhow*
  insane, sprightly old: *Wivenhoe*
  loathesome, merry old:
    Boothby Graffoe
  pompous old: *Ainderby Steeple*

builders
  bottoms of: *Ravenna*
  murderous: *Hodnet*
  rubble-removing techniques of:
    Shottle

bulbs
  light: *Fring*
  that die when you look at
    them: *Lutton Gowts*

bulges
  cheesy: *Eriboll*
  huge, erotic: *Humby*
  medium-sized, erotic: *Huby*
  persistent, unwanted: *Lower
    Peover*
  prestressed: *Bromsgrove*
  pustular: *Bilbster*
  tiny, erotic: *Budby*
  unwelcome, obvious: *Stebbing*

bumps
  in slimming biscuits: *Naples*
  on plastic trays: *Bolsover*

bunches, useless: *Burton Coggles*

buns: *Brymbo*

burglars: *Taroom*

burns, nonpoetic: *Hutlerburn*

buses
  coats on: *Moffat*
  Italian, overdue: *Stagno di Gumbi*
  oversized: *Articlave*
  parts of: *Edgbaston*

buttons
  bacony: *Beccles*
  conversations which feature
    views on: *Gussage*
  tummy: *Lowestoft*

C

cabers, misthrown: *Camer*

cable cars, desires aroused by:
  Abercrave

cafés, nasty: *Cromarty*

cameras
  problems buying: *Ainsworth,
    Hotagen*
  wrong: *Hosmer*

candles, deformed: *Slubbery*

cans
  aerosol, rattly: *Millinocket*
  tin: *Boscastle*

cardboard
  boxes, satisfying: *Kentucky*
  insane amount of: *Dorridge*
  prematurely discarded:
    Nottage
  wedges of folded: *Ludlow*

cards
  identity, loss of: *Margate*
  leaving, insincerity of:
    Berriwillock
  that have to be removed:
    Rickling

carol singers, avoidance of: *Fulking*

carpets
  rucked up edges of: *Thurnby*

things found on: *Silloth*
things littered on: *Blitterlees*

cars
apalling expense of repairing:
Squibnocket
apallingly noisy: *Zumbo*
berks in: *Noak Hoak*
chasing each other: *Imber*
fat chance of getting anywhere
useful in: *Brindle*
fat chance of getting into:
Dalfibble
fat chance of getting your coat
clean again after being in:
Fladderbister
huddled on highways: *Grimbister*
invisible bits of: *Stibbard*
parked, honking at: *Tooting Bec*
steering wheels of: *Tarabulus*
things found under seats of:
Belper
traveling, producing gibberish:
Addis Ababa
unhuddled on highways: *Jalingo*
unsecured contents of: *Scackleton*

cartoons
cheaply produced effects in:
Drumsna
conveniently situated pieces of
vegetation in: *Grimmet*
expressions of faces of characters in: *Ghent*
sparing use of: *Great Tosson*
sudden turns effected in: *Zigong*

carts, rogue: *Motspur*

casserole
elk liver, Swedish: *Skannerup*
week-old, dried: *Pott Shrigley*

cavities
definitely unhygienic: *Glutt
Lodge, Henstridge*
probably unhygienic: *Mankinholes*

ceilings
elderly decorations still on:
Chenies

geniuses not getting on with:
Stagno di Gumbi

celebrities
camp: *Melbury Bubb*
conspicuous: *Sloothby*

chairs
dismantled: *Blitterlees*
marks left by wickerwork:
Kettering
plastic, sweaty: *Skibbereen*
plastic, wheezing: *Essendine*

**chambermaids, grisly discoveries
of:** *Bedfont*

change
bacon-saving: *Nupend*
ice-cream mistaken for small:
Blean
name: *Aalst, Abert*
naughty business with: *Bindle*
octaves at the last moment:
Detchant
of mind about where to eat:
Yonder Bognie
small, wet: *Goole*
small: *Boolteens*

charm
infuriatingly overendowed with:
Offord Darcy, Draffan
lack of: *Winster*
resistant to: *Udine*
woolly, distant: *Sheppey*

cheek
astonishment at one's own:
Coodardy
movements of: *Humber*
noise made by: *Garvock*
noise made while kissing:
Kabwum

cheerful
about to become a bit more:
Mointy
manner of arising from bed:
Spreakley
manner of bouncing on bed:
Abwong

manner of going to Cornwall:
Offleyhoo

cheese
burnt bubble of: *Eriboll*
cottage: *Berkhamsted*
grater, unwashed: *Abinger*
various sizes of: *Fraddam*

chefs, loud wallies who call for them: *Haugham*

chess: *Bishop's Caundle*

chewing gum: *Belper*

children
small, bouncing: *Dunster*
small, demanding of attention:
Nazeing
small, in glasses: *Goginan*
small, inconvenient: *Glassel*
small, reminiscent of Jackson
Pollock: *Polyphant, Smearisary*
small, rude, innocent: *Sneem*
small, sticky: *Badgebup*
small, untalented: *Papcastle*
small, with long legs: *Abruzzo*
small, yelling: *Timble*

chocolates: *Bolsover, Cannock Chase*

chuckles, chummy: *Lybster*

chumminess, man-to-man:
Tillicoultry

cigarettes
in lager, ends of : *Slumbay*
meaningless rituals involving:
Pocking
problems of smoking untipped:
Scopwick
unfairly acquired:
Winston-Salem

cinema
just three minutes from this:
Yonder Bognie
people who've just been to the:
Lowther
seats, monopolization of:
Rochester

swaying about in: Imber,
Ossining

cleaning ladies
conversations to avoid having
with: *Clabby*
preempting: *Spofforth*

cleaning, dry: Knaptoft

cleavages
in bottoms: *Ravenna*
speleological, monstrous:
Simprim

clever
architecturally: *Articlave*
but lazy: *Ible*
decreasingly: *Mogumber*
tactics, useless: *Aboyne*

clifftops
silly little kids on: *Caarnduncan*
noise issuing from: *Craboon*

Clingfilm: *Amlwch*

clippers
gaff-rigged: *Kanturk*
pointless, wielded by ticket
collector: *Didcot*

clocks
alarm, faulty: *Duleek*
alarm, unnecessary: *Dunster*
cuckoo: *Penge*

clots, mad, patronizing: *Largoward*

codgers
boring, famous, old: *Boothby
Graffoe*
huge, wobbling, wheezing, old:
Kingston Bagpuise
stuffy, medieval, old: *Warleggan*

coffee
not quite enough: *Pidney*
noxious substances in:
Cadomin

coffee-machines, intelligent:
Uttoxeter

coins
domestic, much needed: *Nupend*

foreign, assorted: *Boolteens*
foreign, unwanted: *Bindle*

cold
ears, hearty feelings induced by:
Luffness
swimming pool, nearly brave
enough to dive into: *Parbold*
third recurrence of winter: *Snoul*
taps, hot and, deft handling of:
Alltami

collections
awful record: *Hextable*
charity: *Ardelve*
eccentric: *Aldclune*
somnambulent: *Abatolampy*

color
ballpoints, three-: *Ospringe*
depressingly wrong: *Gretna Green*
multi-purpose, municipal:
Frating Green
of paints in catalogs: *Wasp Green*
red, virulent: *Buldoo*
supplements, hideous contents
of: *Mapledurham*

combs, clogged: *Haselbury Plucknett*

commissionaires
boring: *Clabby*
swinish: *Margate*

complaints
tiresome: *Mogumber*
very tiresome: *Ainderby Quernhow*

components
small, meaningless: *Pimlico*
vital, missing: *Exeter*

concepts
hitherto unnamed: *Liff*
that people won't grasp
perfectly simple: *Osbaston*

confetti
overabundance of: *Pathstruie*
royal: *Didcot*

containers
Chinese meal: *Wubin*
ludicrously misnamed: *Sadberge*
contest, bagpipe: *Spittal of Glenshee*

contributions
negligible: *Spoffard*
very public, probably negligible:
Ardelve

conversations
desired: *Affcot*
gaps in: *Samalaman*
interminable: *Ditherington*
polite, interminable: *Clabby*
polite, pointless: *Sittingbourne*
shifting: *Glenties*
thuggish: *Jawf*
wasted: *Harpenden*

cords
electrical, that get pulled back:
Lynwilg
swimming-trunk, that get lost:
Lubcroy

corridors
cowardly behavior in:
Corriecravie
etiquette in: *Corriearklet*
hideous mistimings in:
Corriemoillie
making a mess of walking
down: *Corriemuchloch*
pretending to be Richard Briers
in: *Corriedoo, Corrievorrie*

cosies
spare-toilet-roll: *Ossett*
tee: *Kitmurvy*

cottages
retirement: *Duncraggon*
weekend: *Hull*

coughs
gurgling: *Brisbane*
that don't seem to have any
effect: *Gulberwick*
throaty: *Dorchester*

couples
    arguing loudly: *Heanton Punchardon*
    arguing most of the time: *Badachonacher*
    arguing silently: *Famagusta*
    no longer arguing: *Manitoba*
    pretending not to be arguing: *Nyarling*

cows
    journeys through: *Wendens Ambo*
    things left in fields by: *Munderfield*

craftwork: *Dalrymple*

cravat, worn by Scottish actors: *Glenduckie*

crazy, you don't have to be, etc.: *Snitterfield*

cream
    antiwrinkle: *Melton Constable*
    ice: *Badgebup*

creeps
    boring: *West Wittering*
    about identity of: *East Wittering*

crimes, ancient: *Burlingjobb*

crises, humorous exploitation of: *Gribun*

cross
    a road too slowly: *Sturry*
    a road, not about to: *Bozeman*
    activities indulged in while: *Burleston*
    things that make you: *Draffan, Hickling*
    with zebra: *Yebra*

crossings
    pedestrian: *Bozeman*
    train: *Trantlemore*

crotches, trouser: *Botley, Piddletrenthide*

crouches, upward: *Hucknall*

cry
    end of a: *Mointy*
    ill-equipped to: *Hankate*
    reason to: *Babworth*

cubicles
    inaccessible: *Milwaukee*
    horribly soiled: *Wyoming*

cupboards
    bathroom, attempts to lure people out of: *Visby*
    jugs in: *Upottery*
    kites in: *Kanturk*
    saucepans in: *Cong*
    skeletons in: *Glemanuilt*

curses, Scottish: *Aird of Sleat*

cushions, roadside: *Edgbaston*

customs, charming pointless old: *Edgbaston*

D

Damocles, the Trewoofe of: *Trewoofe*

dances
    in street: *Droitwich, Stelling Minnis*
    of beer glasses: *Sketty*
    people who won't ask people for: *Peening Quarter*
    Polynesian, that the Queen has to sit through: *Grutness*

dearies
    lovable, mad old: *Bradworthy*
    soporific, rabbity old: **Clabby**

decisions
    minor, agonizing: *Deventer*
    right, agonizing: *Abalemma*
    wrong, agonizing: *Huna*

decorations, Christmas: *Clovis, Chenies*

dentists
    activities of unemployed: *Beccles*

results of going to: *Gallipoli,*
Gipping

departures
    inability to make: *Foffarty*
    of madmen: *Throckmorton*
    welcome, of others: *Nubbock*

deposits
    crystalline: *Libenge, Klosters*
    pink, sticky: *Glud*
    sludgy: *Cromarty*
    small, black, satisfying: *Tidpit*

desks
    useful things that fall off: *Tampa*
    useless things that stay on:
      Kilvaxter

desperation
    polite: *Iping*
    frankly rushed: *Wyoming*

determination
    bloody-minded: *Oswestry*
    politely restrained: *Kent, Calicut,*
      Smarden

devices
    agricultural: *Jarrow*
    humorous: *Barstibley*
    immensely complex: *Uttoxeter*

dialogue, single page of: *Clackavoid*

diaries, meaningless entries in:
    Epsom

diarrhea, verbal: *Ainderby Steeple,*
    Spurger

dice: *Hoggeston*

direction
    almost certainly the wrong:
      Brindle
    opposite: *Zigong, Droitwich*
    without any apparent: *Chimkent*

directions, difficulties of
    remembering: *Dinder*

dirt
    on overalls of fraudulent
      workmen: *Podebrady*
    types of: *Sutton and Cheam*

disco
    people who should have been
      left in the: *Hagnaby*
    people who skulk in corners of
      the: *Peening Quarter*

discrepancies, unaccountable:
    Bodmin

diseases
    conveniently debilitating: *Patkai*
      Bum
    of plants, artificial: *Breckles*
    of plants, likely to be induced:
      Lutton Gowts
    unrecognized by medical
      science: *Yalardy, Leazes*

dishwashers: *Dobwalls*

dog-owners, cretinous: *Dogdyke*

dogs
    large, randy, teatime: *Scrabster*
    neat deposits made by French:
      Joliette
    small, moribund: *Scamblesby*
    small, repulsive, snuffling:
      Scorrier
    small, vicious, yappy: *Baughurst*

doors
    carelessly closed car:
      Fladderbister
    deliberately obstructive:
      Ramsgate
    elevator: *Emsworth*
    lockless: *Wyoming, Milwaukee*
    revolving, overpopulated:
      Shifnal
    things caused by walking into:
      Sluggan
    things precariously balanced
      above: *Trewoofe*

doorstep, people you don't want to
see on your: *Corfu*

doubleglazing, inhabitants of:
    Harbottle

drawbridges, mischievously raised:
    Araglin

E

drawers
    bottom: *Marlow*
    things found in: *Pimlico, Burton Coggles*

dressing tables
    small coins found on: *Boolteens*
    things found on hotel: *Lamlash*

dribble
    infantile: *Halcro*
    somnolent: *Sompting*
    waxy: *Slubbery*

drink
    feigned reluctance to: *Alcoy*
    nipping off for a quick: *Lochranza*
    philosophical state during: *Solent*

drinks
    effects of respectable: *Richmond*
    repellent: *Aasleagh, Naas*
    small, long-lasting: *Stody*
    spilt: *Tulsa*

drips
    gooey, waxen: *Slubbery*
    paint: *Zod*

droplets
    hanging, stylish: *Berry Pomeroy*
    hanging, mobile: *Longniddry*
    persistent, trouser: *Wimbledon*

drunks
    methods of detecting: *Tolstachaolais*
    peckish: *Pott Shrigley*
    unappealing: *Pleeley*
    uncomprehending: *Blithbury*

dry, not very: *Wrabness*

duffers, barking mad old: *Pant-Y-Wacco*

dwarves, nubile: *Forsinain*

ears
    fears concerning: *Loberia*
    inner: Nanhoron, *Ulting*
    outer: *Luffness*

earthquakes, humorous: *Drumsna*

edicts, ancient: *Farduckmanton*

eggs
    boiled: *Symond's Yat*
    coffee drunk from receptacle designed for: *Snover*
    scrambled: *Cloates Point*

eighty-year-olds, bounding, refrigerated: *Wivenhoe*

elbows
    damp: *Listowel*
    sexually active, sore: *Bures*
    territorially intrusive: *Rochester*

emotions
    angry, unmusical: *Burleston*
    cheerful: *Spreakley, Abwong*
    infinitely sad: *Glasgow*
    susceptibility of: *Cahors*
    triste: *Sloinge*

ends
    damp, cigarette: *Slumbay*
    long, thin, dangling: *Ranfurly*
    of desks, uses of: *Thrupp*
    of parties: *Aasleagh, Naas*
    of recalcitrant pieces of cotton: *Vidlin*
    of toothbrushes: *Pibsbury*

engineers, telephone, inexplicable marriages to: *Lydiard Tregoze*

entries
    meaningless, in diaries: *Epsom*
    noisy: *Tananarive*
    to Mecca: *Multan*
    to the Kingdom of Heaven: *Vidlin*

envelopes
    dangerous: *Scramoge*
    deceitful: *Hugglescote*
    empty: *Cannock Chase*

environments
    dark, moist: *Huttoft*
    urban, excremental: *Bromsgrove*

epaulettes, useless: *Trossachs*

epiglottis, giant, waggling:
    Ullingswick

erasers, rubber: *Tampa*

Eskimo, sore thumbs of an:
    Anantnag

evenings
    Friday, noisy: *Framlingham*
    tense: *Heanton Punchardon*
    wasted: *Lowther*

events, lack of: *Chimkent*

ex-girlfriend
    new boyfriend of: *Rudge*
    wife's resentment of: *Mavis
        Enderby*

excreta, airborne: *Burlingjobb*

excuses
    feeble: *Dorridge*
    impromptu, but still feeble:
        Hastings
    incredible, unnecessary: *Falster*
    indignant: *Hoff*
    ludicrous: *Brisbane*
    transparent: *Bilbster*

exorcism: *Clenchwarton*

experiences
    hitherto unnamed: *Liff*
    horrific: *Maaruig*
    lurching: *Bedfont*
    melancholy: *Glasgow*
    panicky: *Ditherington*
    satisfying: *Skellow*
    terrific: *Nempnett Thrubwell*

experts, humiliating the: *Aboyne*

expressions
    facial, agonized: *Minchinhampton*
    peculiar: *Banff*

pissed: *Blithbury*
    raging: *Damnaglaur*
    sly: *Golant*
    vaguely attentive: *Hove*

eyebrows
    things that grow between: *Tew*
    useless employment of: *Epping*

F

faces
    besmirched: *Badgebup*
    guilty-looking: *Peru, Hastings*
    silly: *Leeming, Banff*
    warm and salty: *Moisie*

family
    arguments, odd behavior
        during: *Gress*
    fictional, head of: *Potarch*
    hats that don't belong to the:
        Tweedsmuir
    Royal, head of the, being stoic
        in Indonesia: *Grutness*
    Royal, joke-telling privileges of
        the: *Princes Risborough*
    Royal, member of foreign, on
        uppers: *Zlatibor*
    Royal, sleeping with members
        of the: *Randers*
    Royal, understandable fears
        suffered by members of
        the: *Loberia*
    seaside-visiting: *Molesby*

farts—see under NOISES (if you
    must)

fat
    books: *Great Tosson*
    chance of actually winning
        £10,000: *Hugglescote*
    ends of ties: *Ranfurly*
    people: *Humber*
    solicitors: *Valletta*

fears
    anatomical: *Loberia*
    vegetable: *Peoria*

feelings
in unexpected parts of body:
Acklins
of fillings: *Tingrith*
of something or other,
profound: *Hambledon*
queasy: *Guernsey*
queasy, bottom-orientated:
Shoeburyness
sentimental: *Glasgow*
sofa-threatening: *Pollatomish*
tired, cold, thirsty: *Luffenham*
uneasy: *Dungeness, Frating Green*

feet
damp, pink, highly wrinkled:
Dewlish
elephantine, umbrellas for use
of: *Clackmannan*
painful: *Nipishish*
tingling sensations in: *Gilling*
with highly developed tap
skills: *Polbathic*

fencing: *Pabbay*

festoonment: *Chipping Ongar*

fifteen years
at the same desk: *Brough Sowerby*
younger than you, people who
are: *Glasgow*

films
pornographic: *Papworth Everard*
rewritten ends of famous:
Epworth
that won't get made: *Spiddle*

fingers
definitely not green: *Lutton Gowts*
insertion of, into: *Cannock Chase*
lecherous: *Farrancassidy, Tullynessle*
not within reach of: *Nad*
things that cling to: *Mummelgum,
Ardslignish, Dipple*

fish
tropical, stupid: *Stoke Poges*
overabundance of heads of:
Chimbote

flames
almost completely

forgotten old:
Mavis Enderby
people you wish were old:
Lydiard Tregoze
reminders of old: *Mavesyn
Ridware*

flaps
clothy, roomy: *Moffat*
hairy, sparse: *Scraptoft*
increasingly wet and muddy:
Fladderbister
leathery: *Luppitt*

flats
grimy: *Torlundy*
too far from the shops:
Nantwich

Fleming, Sir Alexander: *Eriboll*

flies: *Harbottle*

floor matting, indelicate uses of:
Bures

fluff
mysterious: *Knaptoft*
navel: *Lowestoft*
yellow: *Memphis*

folds
bothersome: *Tolob*
fleshy: *Lusby*
silky: *Shrenk*

food
ethnic, inedible: *Chimbote*
inappropriate: *Kowloon*
misnamed: *Slabberts*
railway, inedible: *Amlwch*
sculptable: *Hepple*
shortly going to be inedible:
Cloates Point
unequal divisions of:
Finuge very little actual,
packets containing: *Dorridge*

footballers, pansy: *Hoddlesdon*

foreigners
impersonation of: *Aberbeeg*
probably deaf or stupid:
Yarmouth

foreplay
  at a distance: *Visby*
  clumsy: *Meadle*
  reconciliatory: *Manitoba*
  vocal: *Low Ardwello*

fowl-feeding: *Farduckmanton*

freemasons
  banned practices of: *Enumclaw*
  ritual pieces of gristle, use of
    by: *Grimsby*

fridges
  concealed matter in: *Goosnargh*
  concealed matter rediscovered
    three weeks later in: *High
    Offley*
  damp things in: *Nantwich*
  strips of floor next to: *Torlundy*
  teeming with life: *Guernsey*

friends
  or so they would like to think:
    *Peterculter, Ardcrony, Boothby
    Graffoe*
  unmarried: *Canudos*

frowning, important: *Frolesworth*

fruit
  in the manner of: *Hordle*
  stupid overabundance of:
    Limassol
  theft of a single piece of:
    Market Deeping

furniture
  air-expelling: *Essendine*
  bamboo, disintegration of:
    Blitterlees
  execrable: *Mapledurham*
  lavatorial: *Osset*

G

Gable, Clark: *Epworth*

games
  ball: *Hoddlesdon, Pelutho*
  board: *Bishop's Caundle, Hoggeston*

  indoor: *Aboyne*
  outdoor, Eastern European:
    Twomileborris

gardening
  equipment, piece of,
    mysterious: *Haxby*
  hopelessness of: *Crail*
  trousers used for: *Broats*

gardens
  alarming sheds in: *Low
    Eggborough*
  embarrassing talks in: *Ambleside*

garments
  discussions about making:
    Gussage
  ethnic, inapposite: *Nokomis*
  exotic, pretentious: *Shalunt*
  fatuous, foreign: *Valletta*
  funny one that man's wearing:
    Roosebeck
  gaberdine, ankle-length:
    Flodigarry
  loose, hateful, well-intentioned:
    Anjozorobe
  naff material for making: *Joplin*
  peculiar, frightful: *Neen Sollars*
  preposterous: *Zafrilla*
  removed with dispiriting
    results: *Wartnaby*
  semi-inverted: *Hessle*
  that don't fool anybody: *Ompton*
  too loose: *Shrenk*
  woolen, knee-length: *Jurby*

gazes, shrewd, berkish: *Wroot*

genitals
  moist: *Wetwang*
  moved about by owner: *Grobister*
  moved about by selves: *Tingewick*
  solitary recreational uses of:
    Southwick, Sloinge
  washed politely: *Paradip*
  well-groomed: *Spruce Knob*

**gestures, ambiguous but bloody
  rude**: *Fovant*

gibberish
    argumentative: *Inverinate*
    nocturnal: *Burslem*
    telephonic: *Harpenden,*
        Gammersgill
    that issues from cars: *Addis*
        Ababa

gin, price of: *Le Touquet*

girlfriend
    long forgotten except by wife:
        Mavis Enderby
    resentment concerning: *Rudge*

girls
    coiffured: *Aubusson*
    naff epistolary habits of: *Ocilla*
    pot-brandishing: *Kittybrewster*
    teenage, in bedroom: *Tibshelf*

gizmos
    plastic, metal, Bakelite: *Pimlico*
    small, clever: *Uttoxeter*
    tasteless: *Barstibley*

glances
    humorous, at blobs: *Swanage*
    meaningful: *Balemartine*

glass
    pointless scraping at: *Quenby*
    pointless tapping on: *Stoke Poges*

globules, yellow, gummy,
unpleasant: *Mugeary*

go
    bbddbbddbbrrbrrrrddrr, things that:
        Thrupp
    off, alarms that don't: *Duleek*
    people who finally: *Nubbock*
    people who just won't: *Clunes*
    to the lavatory, urgent need to:
        Great Wakering
    trying unsuccessfully to: *Foffarty*

goats
    jocular tedious old: *Barstibley*
    noisy tuneless old: *Royston*

golfing, overpaid twats who go:
    Kitmurvy

golf strokes, homicidal: *Whaplode*
    Drove

goo
    sea gull: *Sutton and Cheam*
    waxy: *Slubbery*

good-byes, premature:
    Hidcote Bartram

gossip
    bubbling with: *Malaybalay*
    judicious applications
        of: *Marytavy*
    subject of immense amount of:
        Tukituki

gourmets, slithery: *Berry Pomeroy*

grass
    absence of: *Abruzzo*
    intelligent forms of: *Trispen*

gravel
    infuriating: *Crail*
    walking barefoot on: *Nipishish*

grids, cattle: *Humber*

grocers, green: *Halifax, Smisby*

ground
    things buried four feet in the:
        Pymble
    toxic waste-: *Caarnduncan*
    up: *Sadberge*
    worn away: *Abruzzo*

groups
    infuriatingly indecisive:
        Lowther
    of five that should be four:
        Lampeter
    peer: *Caarnduncan*
    that exclude you: *Margaretting Tye*

guards, railway: *Galashiels*

guilt
    powerful: *Glemanuilt*
    surprised: *Peru*

gumboots
    cold: *Luffness*
    wet: *Burwash*

gunge
    crystalline: *Libenge*
    damp, gummy: *Deal*
    green, shrubby: *Sadberge*
    pinkish: *Glud*
    unwholesome: *Mummelgum*

gurgling
    involuntary, abdominal: *Tumby*
    perfectly reasonable explanation
        for: *Brisbane*
    through straws: *Pitlochry*

gusto, terrific, tuneless: *Royston*

**gutters, dog's business clogging up
the:** *Dogdyke*

H

hair
    armpit, ruffled: *Kimmeridge*
    facial, bizarre: *Scethrog*
    few last strands of: *Scraptoft*
    greasy, legal: *Glazeley*
    paint damage caused by:
        Garrow
    plucking of nostril: *Yonkers*
    pubic, in moussaka: *Scroggs*
    sprigs of, for chasing ants:
        Monks Toft
    tufty interocular bits of: *Tew*
    unaccompanied: *Albacete*
    unbecoming styles of: *Aubusson,*
        Ugglebarnby, Papigochic

handlebar mustaches, female:
    Lossiemouth

hands
    clammy: *Meath*
    psychologically helpful move-
        ments of the: *Scosthrop*
    rubbed: *Ardentinny*
    slimy: *Scurlage*

hangovers, incapacitating:
    Duntish

hankies
    lack of: *Hankate*
    peered into: *Massachusetts*
    worn knotted on head: *Sidcup*

hat behind, leaving one's: *Hidcote
Bartram*

hatred, violent, by spouse: *Mavis
Enderby*

hats
    furry, absurd: *Glinsk*
    gigantic, conical, coolie: *Valletta*
    large, ill-fitting collection of:
        Tweedsmuir
    naff: *Sidcup*

heads
    alarming numbers of fish:
        Chimbote
    black: *Quabbs*
    of state, poorly: *Patkai Bum*

**healthy, hopeless attempts to
become:** *Berkhamsted, Elgin,
Kingston Bagpuise*

**hedge, things to do behind one's
front:** *Todber*

herring, fishermen: *Flodigarry*

highways
    not to be confused with
        madmen on: *Gastard*
    sudden outbreaks of cones on:
        Skagway
    sudden outbreaks of law-
        abiding behavior on:
        Grimbister
    sudden outbreaks of lunch on:
        Strassgang
    sudden outbreaks of reckless
        joyfulness on: *Jalingo*

history, lost in the mists of:
    Hutlerburn

holes
    bath overflow: *Polperro*
    in ballpoint pens: *Pluvigner*
    in toothbrushes: *Pibsbury*

things which get stuck over:
Spuzzum
things which settle into: *Writtle*
things which sit on: *Dillytop*

holidays
impressively unencumbered:
Nuncargate
naïve behavior on: *Valletta*
not won in competitions:
Shalunt
people met on: *Corfu*
things brought home from:
Glassel, Jubones, Anjozorobe

home
at BBC Radio studios, birds
that make their: *Waccamaw*
people who'd rather go: *Lowther*
stuff that turns up in your:
Mavesyn Ridware
things that don't look good at:
Jubones
things that happen on the way:
Heanton Punchardon
things that might be at:
Mankinholes
time to go: *Inigonish*

hooks
jammy: *Halcro*
picture, things for banging in:
Nogdam End

hopefulness
misplaced, of being amusing:
Gaffney
naïve, regarding lunch: *Jeffers*
naïve, regarding tea: *Teigngrace*
of finding idiot: *Kibblesworth*
of getting better invitation:
Darvel

horns
large, uncomfortable: *Humby*
long, ceremonial: *Hunsingore*
moderate-sized, but unconceal-
able: *Huby*
small, Scandinavian:
Oswaldtwistle

horror
conversational: *Wigan*
inexpressible: *Maaruig*

horses
china, rude: *Barstibley*
understandably irate: *Belding*

hostesses, airline: *Ewelme*

hotels
incredibly dull things in:
Lamlash
mock-Tudor: *Melcombe Regis*
shambolic, clanking: *Bonkle*

houses
dolls': *Tewel*
opera, spittle in: *Ullapool*
rented: *Delaware*
romantic doo-doos in reptile:
Dunbar
rubble removals from: *Shottle*
strange, dark: *Islesteps*
strange, noisy: *Whissendine*
things in the cellar of: *Tanvats*
White, amnesiacs in: *Esterhazy*

hunches, foolish, in the theater:
Totteridge

hutlers, clumsy: *Hutlerburn*

hymns
pitched at random: *Royston*
pitched too high or low:
Detchant

I

ice, octogenarians under the:
Wivenhoe

idea
having a better: *Ferfer*
not having the faintest:
Epsom, Osbaston
very much his own: *Brough
Sowerby*

identity cards, left at home:
  Margate

idiots
  roaring, pretentious: *Haugham*
  ludicrous, deluded: *Kibblesworth*

implements
  curious, horticultural: *Haxby*
  useless: *Ipplepen*
  wooden, silly: *Ibstock*

income tax, impossibility of under-
standing: *Swanibost*

incontinence, reptilian: *Dunbar*

infants, small, naked, comical:
  Barstibley

informative, disinclined to be:
  Clixby

inklings, tiny, stomach-curdling:
  Ely

interesting
  how: *Nome*
  mildly: *Scugog*
  temporarily: *Glassel*
  than you, someone more:
   Sconser
  than your newspaper, more:
   Corfe

interval
  eight-month: *Peterculter*
  theater bars in the: *Tabley*
   Superior

into each other
  bumping: *Droitwich*
  things that go: *Toronto*

invitations
  obligatory: *Oughterby*
  waited for: *Darvel*

items
  nasal, airborne: *Scronkey*
  prunelike, waterlogged: *Dewlish*
  sticky, clammy: *Belper*
  sticky, furry: *Silloth*
  thin, circular, meaty: *Shanklin*

J

jackets
  dust: *Pulverbatch*
  hairy, stained: *Bradford*
  hideous casual: *Saffron Walden*
  loud check: *Louth*
  not quite long enough: *Stebbing*
  things found in: *Nupend*

jam
  canteen, semidelicious
   ingredients of: *Masberry*
  jars, coverings for: *Jid*
  not worth stealing: *Fremantle*
  used for fastening clothes:
   Halcro

jogging, suicide by means of :
  Kingston Bagpuise

jokes
  decreasingly funny: *Gignog*
  early warnings of ends of:
   Pontybodkin
  length of: *Gildersome*
  medieval, practical: *Araglin*
  mild for vicars: *Bude*
  practical, spectacular: *Banteer*
  technically inept: *Jofane*
  told to wrong audience:
   Saucillo
  well-received: *Smyrna*

judges, things they have to put up
  with: *Dockery, Glazeley*

K

keys
  car, endless inability to find:
   Dalfibble
  useless bunches of: *Burton Coggles*

kilts, hoary old gags about:
  Glenwhilly

kindness, unconvincing forms of:
  Frutal

kiss

    musical accompaniment to: *Kabwum*

    performed while chewing gum: *Oystermouth*

kitchens

    incomprehensible technology in: *Pingaring*

    walls of: *Smearisary*

knees

    soreness of due to rock and roll: *Dattuck*

    soreness of due to sex: *Bures*

knights

    frequent: *Dubbo*

    teased: *Araglin*

    wet: *Bealings*

knives

    fish, other uses for: *Botswana*

    muddled up with forks: *Fentonadle*

knobs

    medium-size: *Belper*

    pointless, stony: *Plympton*

knots

    in handkerchieves: *Sidcup*

    intricate: *Kanturk*

L

ladies, cleaning: *Clabby*

laughter

    awkward absence of: *Umberleigh*

    hearty, false: *York*

    loyal: *Princes Risborough*

    tactical: *Swanage*

lavatories

    hats in downstairs: *Tweedsmuir*

    insufficient willy-waggling in: *Piddletrenthide, Botley*

    juvenile behavior in: *Tincleton*

keenness to visit: *Iping*

    misleading stains acquired in: *Botley*

    panic preceding visits to: *Great Wakering*

    search for unstained: *Wyoming*

    things you shouldn't be doing in: *Skulamus*

    unsightly: *Klosters*

lawnmowers, frustrated: *Trispen*

leathery flapping bits: *Luppitt*

Leeds, hotels in: *Absecon*

legs

    extremely unwelcome things up: *Scrabster*

    false, improvised: *Ludlow*

    things not underneath: *High Limerigg*

    things underneath: *Hucknall*

    unwelcome things down: *Wimbledon*

    unwelcome things on: *Polloch*

    unwelcome things up: *Affpuddle*

    useless: *Clun*

    welcome things up: *Burwash*

letters

    deceptively enticing: *Hugglescote*

    French: *Phillack*

    important: *Morangie*

    incomprehenisble: *Dalderby*

licking of envelopes: *Scramoge*

lids

    noises caused by: *Balzan*

    things immediately beneath: *Jid*

    useless for putting on things, apparently antique: *Lydd*

life

    state of your: *Shimpling*

    the British Way of: *Botcherby*

    the facts of: *Ambleside*

    uneventfulness of: *Chimkent*

lifts

    heavy breathing in: *Burbage*

misuse of by weeds: *Nybster*

silence in: *Emsworth*

light bulbs

dazedness caused by: *Lampung*

needing to be disposed of: *Fring*

problems of disposing of:
Clathy

limp

arm, thespian: *Oundle*

bogus, sporting: *Hoddlesdon*

bread: *Yate*

lines

wavy: *Ghent*

literary critics: *Ripon*

loaves, curious-shaped: *Bradworthy*

lobby, great oafs screeching in the:
Haugham

looks

frosty: *Gartness*

lecherous: *Frosses*

superior, at shoes: *Dubuque*

superior, in theater: *Tabley
Superior*

warning: *Balemartine*

wistful, unexplained: *Foping*

lost

in any one of a number of
places: *Kelling*

in the grass: *Rimbey*

in the mists of history:
Hutlerburn

in the photocopier: *Dufton*

objects that turn up: *Winkley*

perpetually: *Dalfibble*

quickly becoming: *Brindle*

loudness

of apologies: *Hickling*

of declaimed opinions: *Prague*

of gurgling: *Pitlochry*

of jacket: *Louth*

of nocturnal noises: *Taroom,
Bonkle*

of voice: *Rufforth, Yarmouth,
Haugham, Lulworth*

lounges, cocktail: *Melcombe Regis*

love, unrequited: *Lydiard Tregoze*

luggage

economical with: *Nuncargate*

ill-behaved: *Adlestrop*

lumps

agricultural, aromatic: *Jarrow*

awkward, in trousers: *Stebbing*

cardboard, useful: *Ludlow*

disgusting, attached to face:
Kirby

dull, in suitcase: *Glassel*

edible, steaming, irremovable:
Glossop

gristly, acrid: *Grimsby*

gummy, shapeless: *Papcastle*

powdery, floating: *Poges*

small, awkward, dangerous:
Fraddam

small, nasal: *Peebles*

tiny, in swimming trunks:
Lubcroy

unwelcome, nocturnal, in front:
Humby

unwelcome, nocturnal,
underneath: *Tolob*

unwelcome, urban, all over:
Burlingjobb

urban, overhead and underfoot:
Bromsgrove

useless, that stick out: *Zod, Huby*

M

madmen, departed, in toasters:
Throckmorton

make up

kiss and: *Manitoba*

lopsided: *Wollondilly*

manholes, open, amusing: *Frimley*

maneuvers, awkward, leaping: *Hobbs
Cross*

maps, road: *Kalami*

margarine: *Darenth*

markets, super: *Duggleby, Flimby, Motspur, Boscastle*

mats, small, sopping: *Listowel*

matter, gaseous: *Eriboll*

mattresses
banana-shaped: *Baumber*
enormous, muscular: *Harbledown*

maybe, meaning to: *Yesnaby*

meals
arguments about where to have: *Lowther*
arguments at the end of: *Bodmin*
hopelessly overoptimistic: *Jeffers*
light, nutritious, for busy playwrights: *Cresbard*
noises after: *Poona*
things they come in: *Wubin*
to avoid: *Skannerup*

meaningless
components, small: *Pimlico*
holes in brogues: *Tockholes*
letters to editor: *Dalderby*
noises, distant: *Amersham*
smiles, shiny: *Ewelme*

measure of luminosity: *Blean*

measure of time
art galleries: *Frolesworth*
camera shops: *Ainsworth*
elevators: *Emsworth*

measures of distance
parking lots: *Nad*
sheep: *Sheppey*
trousers: *Malibu*
tubes: *Frant*

meat, ghastly surprises in: *Aigburth*

medallions, gold: *Herstmonceux*

memory
attempts to prod into some kind of action: *Memus*
difficulty of getting things to lodge in the: *Dinder*

frustrating behavior of: *Cafu, Fiunary*
loss of in kitchen: *Woking*
loss of in White House: *Esterhazy*
loss of re bruises: *Ampus*

men
dismal, pedantic, little: *Benburb*
pathetic, deluded, little: *Brough Sowerby*
myopic, dangerous, little: *Low Eggborough*

menus
at the end of meal, people who reach for: *Scranton*
bits you can remember of: *Kenilworth*
Muslim: *Albuquerque*

merciless boiling: *Cong*

merry-go-rounds: *Adrigole*

mid-pee, pulling the chain in: *Tincleton*

middle
aged coloraturas: *Ullingswick*
aged ladies: *Lossiemouth*
aged, balding: *Ugglebarnby*
aged, desperate: *Papigochic*
Ages, trousers worn in: *Goosecruives*
class: *Pitroddie*
of night: *Balzan, Lampung*
of nowhere, hairs found in: *Albacete*
of perusal: *Peru*
of Scottish folk song: *Lochranza*

milk jugs, unnecessary numbers of: *Upottery*

mistakes
horrifying, too drunk to avoid: *Hagnaby*
horrifying, unavoidable: *Wigan*

moats: *Bealings*

modesty, false: *Simprim*

moments
    awful: *Umberleigh*
    deeply embarrassing: *Lulworth*
    utterly pant-wetting: *Wembley*

monasteries: *Corstorphine*

moods
    antivegetative: *Hewish*
    irrational: *Cranleigh*
    of deep irritation: *Corriecravie*
    peevish, sofa-destroying:
        Pollatomish
    wavily depicted: *Ghent*

moors: *Luffness, Luffenham, Slogarie*

morning
    after a bagpipe-playing contest:
        Spittal of Glenshee
    after a party: *Picklenash, Silloth*
    bits of you waking up in the:
        Tingewick
    cheerfulness in the: *Spreakley*
    five o'clock in the: *Bonkle*
    horrified awakening in the:
        Maaruig
    nasty shock in the: *Hagnaby*
    stiff and achey in the: *Liniclate*
    surprising appearance in the:
        Sheepy Magna
    three o'clock in the: *Burslem*
    time off in the: *Slipchitsy*
    twenty past nine in the:
        Framlingham
    two o'clock in the: *Pott Shrigley*

**moron, not wanting to be thought
a:** *Frolesworth*

morsels, small, prominent, repulsive: *Kirby*

motorbikes
    feeling of new: *Nempnett
        Thrubwell*
    involuntary impersonation of:
        Berepper

moussaka, stout pubes in: *Scroggs*

movements
    bowel: *Glororum*
    fishlike: *Gipping*
    flabby: *Humber*
    futile, at post offices: *Stoke Poges*
    futile, at waiters: *Epping*
    futile, in own house: *Kelling*
    vague, manual, searching:
        Scosthrop
    waggling, artistic: *Llanelli*

mumbles, deliberate: *Inverkeithing*

**Murmansk, things that shouldn't
be in:** *Glentaggart*

mush, dehydrated: *Pott Shrigley*

music
    rendered weepy by old: *Cahors*
    simple, played badly: *Dinsdale*

N

'n': *Nacton*

names
    being cute with: *Ocilla, Cheb*
    cheating with: *Aalst*
    execrable: *Drebley*
    forgetting of: *Golant, Inverkeithing*
    loves that dare not speak their:
        Lyminster
    sudden reconsidering of: *Abert*

nap
    conditions in which you should
        try to have a: *Duntish,
        Hynish, Cranleigh*
    limbs having a: *Clun*
    things brushed against the:
        Nith

Neapolitan, tubs, fists shoved into:
Blean

needles
    conversations that are largely
        concerned with: *gussage*
    things that won't go through
        the eyes of: *Vidlin*

nerds
conferences for unwanted:
Absecon
excited: *Hugglescote*
incredible little: *Corfu*
piddling, in your lavatory:
Tincleton
preeping: *Widdicombe*
tittering, white-collar: *Snitterby*

New York
cluelessness in: *Lackawanna*
employment opportunities in:
Steenhuffel

news, astounding: *Jawcraig*

newspaper
cuttings, comical: *Snitter*
fascination of someone else's:
Corfe
opinions gleaned from: *Macroy*
proprietors, monstrous:
Bickerstaff
racks, bewildering fascination
with: *Condover*

night
dazedness during: *Lampung*
noises during: *Balzan,*
Whissendine, Bonkle, Boinka
things purloined during:
Ambatolampy

nipples, high profile: *Budby*

nitwits, great steaming: *Duggleby*

no, expressed as yes: *Yesnaby*

nods
surly, from behind hedge: *Todber*
thoughtful, vacant: *Dinder*

nodules
plastic, melted: *Stutton*
rubber: *Pimperne*

noises
bodily, benign: *Bepton*
bubbling and inopportune:
Tumby
burbling and nocturnal: *Bonkle*

discreet but unwelcome: *Affcot*
distant and meaningless:
Amersham
grunting and considerate:
Horton-cum-Studley
gurgling and milky: *Pitlochry*
gushing and cooing: *Oshkosh*
humming and grinding:
Burleston
humming and groaning:
Milwaukee
loud and clattering:
Clackmannan
loud and deafening: *Balzan*
loud and embarrassing:
Berepper
loud and informative: *Taroom*
loud and rattling: *Hoggeston*
loud and revolving: *Cairo*
minuscule, worrying: *Fring*
mumbling, uninterested: *Nazeing*
nocturnal, interminable:
Framlingham
nocturnal, intermittent:
Whissendine
painful and squeaky: *Skibbereen*
post-prandial: *Poona*
quiet and rubbery: *Tampa*
resounding from clifftops:
Craboon
screeching, Celtic: *Lochranza*
screeching, infantile:
Caarnduncan
squeaky, nylonish: *Screeb*
tatatting and satisfying: *Ibstock*
ticketatacketaticketting: *Seattle*
ticketatacktackatuckaticketting:
Trantlemore
triumphant and slappy: *Beppu*
trumpeting, hippopotamoid:
Brompton
warm and underwater: *Budle*
whiffling, in lifts: *Burbage*
whirring and chuntering:
Ipswich

noses
  adornments to: *Botolphs*
  bleeding: *Burton Coggles*
  erstwhile contents of:
    Longniddry
  fascinating items in:
    Massachusetts
  ill-equipped to deal with runny:
    Hankate
  noises made with: *Burbage*
  things which are ejected from:
    Scurlage
  things which come down from:
    Des Moines
  things which stretch a long way
    from: *Coilantogle*
  tools for stuffing into:
    Botusfleming

**nozzles, aircraft, strange powers
  over:** *Ventnor*

numbers
  lost: *Staplow*
  wrong, for any given purpose:
    Pleven
  wrong, or so he claims:
    Kurdistan

O

objects
  banana-shaped: *Baumber*
  bloody-minded: *Ardslignish*
  clammy, inedible: *Amlwch*
  contented stares at: *Dallow,
    Skellow*
  creatively misapplied: *Botswana*
  dangerously misleading: *Pymble*
  deformed: *Duddo*
  elephantine: *Clackmannan*
  fantastically dull: *Lamlash*
  flimsy, intriguing: *Corfu*
  frilly: *Ossett*
  heavy, with toes on: *Clun*
  hidden, pointed: *Gilgit*
  hideous, shelfbound: *Delaware*

  hitherto unnamed: *Liff*
  horribly, roomy: *Mapledurham*
  innocent, repeatedly hit:
    Ashdod
  Kenyan: *Jubones*
  long-handled: *Botusfleming*
  lost, found again: *Winkley*
  massive, wooden, airborne:
    Camer
  plastic, pretensious: *Brumby*
  sticky, jam-infested: *Halcro*
  sticky, permanent: *Dipple*
  sticky, wooden: *Cotterstock*
  strange, culinary: *Cong*
  that don't fool anyone:
    Zeerust
  tiny, disgusting: *Chipping
    Ongar*
  tiny, pointless: *Didcot*
  twelve, baffling: *Cowcaddens*
  unappealing, lonely: *Brymbo*
  wet, cold, enormous: *Trewoofe*
  with bumps on: *Bolsover*
  with holes in, artistic:
    Bromsgrove, Dalrymple

officers, retired, army, raving:
  Pant-y-Wacco

offices
  comical cuttings on walls of:
    Snitter
  fat chance of getting anything
    to work properly in:
    Podebrady
  lost pieces of paper in: *Dufton*
  managers who hide in their:
    Harmanger
  people who decorate: *Clovis,
    Snitterby*
  resentful people in: *Brough
    Sowerby*
  scapegoats in: *Bickerstaff*

officials
  people who become: *Benburb*
  who make your life a misery:
    Margate

olds
> bounding, refrigerated, eighty-year-: *Wivenhoe*
> cringe-making, fourteen-year-: *Cheb*
> on heat, sixteen-year-: *Frosses*
> sweating, forty-year-: *Kingston Bagpuise*

on, trying it: *Brabant*

ooze, yellow: *Clonmult*

opinions
> confident, wrong: *Macroy*
> hard to tolerate: *Chaling*
> that taxi-drivers wish to share with you: *Watendlath, Crieff*
> unasked-for, reverend: *Dean Funes*

orchestra pits, spittle in: *Ullapool*

orchestras
> people who conduct from the audience: *Thrumster*
> that spit a lot: *Ullapool*

orgasm, multiple: *Papworth Everard*

ornaments, misapplied: *Bishop's Caundle*

overalls, inky: *Hibbing*

P

page
> last, of book: *Beppu*
> last, of document, left in photocopier: *Dufton*
> single, blithering: *Clackavoid*

pain and shame: *Yonkers*

pains, sudden: *Acle*

paint smudges, expensive: *Dalrymple*

paintbrushes, cheap: *Aith*

paint stirrers: *Cotterstock*

pajamas
> comforting: *Lambarene*
> Muslim: *Albuquerque*

pangs, terrible: *Lydiard Tregoze*

panic
> in airport: *Hever*
> in corridor: *Ditherington*
> in lavatory: *Great Wakering*

paper
> barely soiled toilet: *Riber*
> silver, against teeth: *Tingrith*
> tangled, spinning: *Strelley*
> under lid: *Jid*

parents
> attempts to mislead: *Shimpling*
> embarrassed: *Sneem*
> god: *Urchfont*
> parties given by: *Frosses*

parking lots, automatic: *Nad*

particles, nasal: *Massachusetts*

parties
> adventurous behavior at: *Hallspill*
> crud under sofas after: *Silloth*
> deposits acquired at curious dinner: *Sutton and Cheam*
> dreadful guests at: *Nubbock, Oughterby*
> frosty glances at dinner: *Inigonish*
> heated recriminations after: *Heanton Punchardon*
> irritatingly successful people at: *Draffan, Offord Darcy*
> people to avoid at: *East Wittering, West Wittering*
> political: *Firebag*
> steamy, teenage: *Frosses*
> things drunk in desparation at end of: *Aasleagh*
> things found in lager cans at the end of: *Slumbay*
> things found in wineglasses after: *Picklenash*
> things removed from rooms before: *Spokane*
> welcome departures from: *Nubbock*

women's conversational exclusiveness at: *Flums*

parts, private, had by dog for lunch: *Scorrier*

patches
wet, under bottom: *Hobbs Cross*
wet, underarm: *Pitsligo*

paving stones: *Affpuddle*

pebbles, wet, shiny: *Glassel*

pedants: *Ainderby Quernhow*

pee
foot-tingling sensations caused by: *Gilling*
inability to do with audience present: *Kettleness*

pellets, unmentionable: *Peebles*

pencil sharpenings, giant: *Blitterlees*

penises
embarrassingly visible, use less: *Huby*
embarrassingly visible: *Stebbing*
hard-working: *Papworth Everard*
inexpertly rendered likenesses of: *Skrubburdnut*
injuries to: *Minchinhampton*
interested: *Tingewick*
lawn-sprinkling mode of: *Spuzzum*
moist: *Wetwang*
obstinate: *Humby*
played with: *Southwick, Sloinge*
politely washed: *Paradip*
regularly moved about: *Grobister*
tent-supporting: *Visby*

pens
lack of: *Aynho*
uselessness of: *Kilvaxter*

people
boring, pairs of: *Mimbridge*
cringing, irritating: *Greeley*

frantic, disorganized: *Worksop*
irritatingly acquiescent: *Dunino*
irritatingly non-acquiescent: *Nindigully*
large groups of helpful grunting: *Horton-cum-Studley*
large groups of miserly: *Bodmin*
medium-sized clumps of enraged: *Dolgellau*
neat old: *Pingandy*
niggling: *Scranton*
reassuring: *Lemvig*
reliably unreliable: *Marytavy*
small families of horrible: *Molesby*
small groups of whiffling: *Burbage*
smooth, greedy: *Winston-Salem*
suspiciously motivated: *Frutal*
underprivileged, leg-wise: *Wigan*
unshaven, maddening: *Draffan*
vast, wobble-cheeked: *Humber*
who give themselves the biggest slice: *Finuge*
who should not be allowed near a piano: *Dinsdale*
wrong-sized groups of: *Lampeter*
you don't want to talk to again: *Staplow*

perpetuity, in: *Cotterstock*

photographs
passport, amusement caused by: *Happas*
passport, expressions worn in: *Banff*

piano
moving: *Nundle*
people who should on no account be allowed near a: *Dinsdale*

picnic spots
> disappointing: *Munderfield*
> infested with wasps: *Swaffham Bulbeck*

pigs, matching: *Tibshelf*

piles, unstable: *Boscastle*

pillows
> clean: *Abilene*
> damp: *Sompting*

pimples, volcanic: *Bilbster*

pins
> danger: *Acle*
> safety: *Lubcroy*

pipers: *Lochranza*

pipes, things hit by: *Ashdod*

places, safe: *Fiunary*

plants
> artificial, diseased: *Breckles*
> sentenced to death: *Lutton Gowts*
> thwacking at: *Hewish*

pleasure, idiosyncratic, revolting: *Glororum*

plugs, bath: *Dillytop, Twomileborris*

plumbers
> could do with a visit from some: *Bonkle*
> ignorance of whereabouts of: *Suckley Knowl*

plumbing noises: *Bonkle*

pockets
> omnivorous: *Nantucket*
> public displays of searching: *Ardelve*
> upholstered: *Hassop*

points, sound made by trains crossing: *Trantlemore*

poles, strong desire to grasp: *Abercrave*

police
> highway snarl-ups caused by: *Grimbister*
> highway snarl-ups eased by: *Jalingo*
> The Leith: *Tolstachaolais*
> what passes for politeness among the: *Surby*

policeman, skin of: *Melton Constable*

politicians
> rabid, left-wing, rich: *Quedgeley*
> ridiculous, furry-hatted: *Glinsk*

politics
> sole contribution to: *Spoffard*
> tiresome: *Firebag*
> unacceptable face of: *Scridain*

poltergeists, resident in car: *Worgret*

poodles, glass: *Tibshelf*

pornography, the making of: *Papworth Everard*

positions, switches which seem to be off in both: *Ockle*

potatoes
> fear of: *Peoria*
> misshapen: *Duddo*

pouches
> small, designer, condom-containing: *Phillack*
> small, humorous: *Glenwhilly*

poultry-keepers: *Goosecruives*

prats, overdressed, incompetent: *Kitmurvy*

prefaces: *Querrin*

pretenses
> absurd: *Dogdyke*
> ingratiating: *Puning*
> intellectual: *Bathel*
> proud: *Prungle*
> seasonal: *Fulking*

prices
>   gin: *Le Touquet*
>   property: *Munster*

problems
>   of disposing of light bulbs:
>   *Clathy*
>   of putting on sweater: *Hessle*

prongs
>   bent: *Bromsgrove*
>   concealed: *Hadzor*
>   clogged with sludge: *Henstridge*
>   truncated: *Baldock*

prunelike extremities: *Dewlish*

pubs
>   berks in: Louth, *Boothby Graffoe*
>   passing time of day in: *Todding*
>   table hoggers in: *Stody*
>   to open, waiting for the:
>   *Luffenham*

puddings, miserable: *Nutbourne*

puddles
>   exterior: *Burwash, Affpuddle*
>   interior: *Goole, Sketty*

punishment, capital, in schools:
>   *Little Urswick*

purpose, unfathomable: *Haxby*

pus, scarlet: *Buldoo*

push taps, embarrassment caused
>   **by:** *Botley*

pushy, people who are: *Brabant*

pyramids, metallic: *Boscastle*

Q

questions
>   expecting answers: *Nome*
>   not expecting answers: *Spurger*
>   not leaving room for answers:
>   *Ainderby Steeple*

queues: *Duggleby, Foindle,*
>   *Twomileborris*

R

races, three-legged: *Shifnal*

radio
>   boring, high-brow: *Meuse*
>   boring, low-brow: *Burslem*
>   boring, middle-brow:
>   *Blandford*
>   *Forum*
>   strange tropical birds on the:
>   *Waccamaw*

raincoats
>   expensive: *Trossachs*
>   uselessness of in rain:
>   *Plenmeller*

rattling, senseless: *Amersham*

reactions, chemical, unedifying:
>   *Bradford*

realizations
>   embarrassing: *Gammersgill,*
>   *Hidcote Bartram*
>   irritating: *Tooting Bec*
>   lurching: *Bedfont*
>   sudden: *Duleek, Dunboyne*

reasons
>   for clipping things, no
>   apparent: *Didcot*
>   for designing bath plug, no
>   accountable: *Dillytop*
>   for naming things, no known:
>   *Sadberge*
>   for sleeping with people,
>   obscure: *Randers*
>   for spray in your mouth,
>   unknown: *Skoonspruit*
>   for staring at something, no
>   particular: *Dallow*

reassurance
>   much needed: *Godalming*
>   spurious: *Old Cassop*

reception
>   chilly: *Saucillo*
>   not very good: *Gweek*

relationships
  unresolved: *Badachonacher*
  wish to sort out other people's:
    Canudos

relevant
  only slightly: *Juwain*
  surprisingly: *Gress*

relish trays: *Clonmult, Sadberge, Buldoo*

reluctance
  feigned, easily overcome:
    Climpy
  feigned, very easily overcome:
    Alcoy

remarks
  calculated, crowd-pleasing:
    Firebag
  own, rather amusing, unheard:
    Dorchester, Umberleigh
  stoicism in the face of
    wounding: *Calicut*

removals
  non-furniture: *Dipple, Grimsby,*
    Rickling, Spokane, Tolob,
    Watendlath, Botusfleming, Crail
  piano: *Nundle*

requests, whining, unwelcome:
    Quall

restaurants
  embarrassing manual behavior
    in: *Ardentinny*
  embarrassing vocal behavior in:
    Haugham
  perverse behavior in: *Kowloon*

revelations, personal with stomach-
  rumble: *Tumby*

Richard III: *Oundle*

rights
  ancient, pebbly: *Pevensey*
  ancient, with midgets: *Forsinain*
  telling lefts from: *Memus, Noak*
    Hoak

ripping, of skin: *Wike*

roads, signposting of: *Botcherby*

rock, small pieces of, apparently
  limitless quantities of: *Crail*

rolls, sausage, stuff you wouldn't
  even find in: *Gruids*

Rowing, accidents while: *Anantnag*

rubbers
  noises made by: *Tampa*
  places for keeping: *Phillack*
  you didn't want to be asked
    about: *Sneem*

rubbish, vital, in dustcart: *Nottage*

rucksacks: *York*

rugs, horse-shoe-shaped, fluffy:
    Luton

rulers, noises made by: *Thrupp*

runs, token: *Naples*

Ryvita, consistency of: *Naples*

S

sachets, impenetrable: *Naugatuck*

sacking: *Tillicoultry*

safe places: *Fiunary*

salami: *Shanklin*

sandwiches
  bacon: *Beccles*
  in London: *Darenth*
  on trains: *Amlwch*

sarong, appearing in lobby wearing
  a: *Valletta*

saucepans
  almost but not quite spotless:
    Radlett
  chocolate-filled: *Abinger*

saunters, carefree: *Frimley*

sausages
  in rolls: *Gruids*
  stuff to smear on: *Patney*
  twisted: *Kerry*

scabs, amorous: *Bures*

schoolteachers: *Bradford*

scissors
> looking for: *Scosthrop*
> other uses for: *Nogdam End*

scones: *Pudsey*

Scotch tape: *Ardslign*

Scotty in Star Trek: *Maaruig*

scribbles: *Screggan*

seaside, by the, firmly locked in car: *Molesby*

seats
> aircraft: *Rochester*
> lavatory: *Luton*

secret
> deliberately badly kept: *Marytavy*
> supposed to be, but who are you trying to kid?: *Tukituki*

secretions, in hamburger joints: *Clonmult*

self-knowledge, serene, completely wrong: *Solent*

sensations, lurching: *Bedfont*

sentences, finishing other people's: *Happle*

services
> church: *Royston, Detchant*
> monastic: *Corstorphine*

seven
> miles of concealed moorland: *Slogarie*
> stomachs, objects passing through: *Wendens Ambo*

sex
> bothersome interruptions of: *Humby*
> could probably do with some: *Pollatomish*
> enjoyed by other people: *Boinka*
> ill-kept secrets about: *Tukituki*

> messes caused by: *Hobbs Cross, Bedfont*
> minor injuries sustained during: *Bures*
> nasty shocks after: *Hagnaby*
> nasty shocks before: *Wartnaby*
> people who want: *Visby, Low Ardwello*
> things that put you off the whole idea of: *Hextable*
> uncertain about: *Libode*

shades of green
> domestic: *Gretna Green*
> institutional: *Frating Green*
> things that clearly should not be included among: *Wasp Green*

shagged out: *Swanibost*

Shakespeare
> working lunches prepared for: *Cresbard*

shaving: *Hathersage*

sheds
> nuclear: *Low Eggborough*
> potting: *Haxby*
> tool: *Cotterstock*

sheep
> mysterious complaints of: *Jawcraig*
> woolly charm of in distance: *Sheppeysheets*
> bloody awful, nylon: *Brecon*
> bottom: *Baumber, Bedfont*

shelves
> hideous stuff on: *Delaware, Tibshelf*
> improvised chess pieces found on: *Bishop's Caundle*

shifting, anxious: *Iping*

shingle, collectors of: *Pevensey*

shirts
> beer down: *Tulsa*
> damp: *Wedderlairs*

open to waist: *Herstmonceux*
stabbing: *Acle*

shoes
bits that hang off: *Luppitt*
perforations in: *Tockholes*
wrong sort of: *Dubuque*

shops
absent companions who turn
up in: *Flagler*
dress: *Dolgellau*
maddening, camera: *Ainsworth*
shoe, idiot: *Kibblesworth*
with stupid names: *Drebley*

shouting at foreigners: *Yarmouth*

showers, agonizing: *Alltami*

sick
feeling in throat after being:
Gulberwick
off wrong side of boat: *Silesia*

side
things on the other: *Quenby*
things that stick out the: *Aith*
things written on the: *Dorridge*

sideburns, extensive, scrofulous:
Galashiels

**signposts, pathetic attempt at
proper:** *Botcherby*

signs, to be taken seriously:
Belding

silences, ghastly: *Lulworth*

singers
awful: *Royston*
carol, hiding from: *Fulking*
wailing: *Lochranza*

single
and proud of it, or so they
claim: *Prungle*
desire to see people stop being:
Canudos
hair: *Albacete*
men who are too groovy to
dance: *Peening Quarter*

six times before, stories heard:
Smarden

sixteen
-year-olds in heat: *Frosses*

skiing: *Zeal Monachorum*

skills
bath-filling: *Alltami*
cowardly: *Corriecravie*
kissing: *Oystermouth*
loaf-naming: *Bradworthy*
useless as it turns out: *Aboyne*

skin
flaps of: *Scopwick*
twists of: *Kerry*
displayed expanses of: *Bogue*

sleep
larcenous behavior during:
Ambatolampy
muck in eyes after: *Mugeary*
people with whom you're not
sure if you want to: *Libode*
things which might help you
get to: *Burslem*
things which prevent you
getting to: *Burleston,
Framlingham*
things which prevent you
staying: *Lostwithiel, Dunster*
things which shouldn't have
gone to: *Clun*

slimming, feeble dishonest shot at:
Berkhamsted

slobs
complete: *Snover*
lazy: *Abinger*

sludge
brittle: *Cromarty*
moist: *Eads*

smells, horrible: *Keele*

smiles
frozen, horrified: *Sneem*
grim, determined: *Smarden*
shiny, meaningless: *Ewelme*

smoking, excuses for: *Brisbane*

smutty postcards: *Snitterfield*

snacks, nasty: *Nantwich*

sneezing
> failure to: *Amersham*
> horribly violent success at:
> > *Scronkey*

snippets, hairy: *Hathersage*

snow, wedges of lurking: *Trewoofe*

soap opera, Australian: *Clackavoid*

socks
> contents of: *Skenfrith*
> things that appear above: *Bogue*

sofa
> restlessly plucked at: *Pollatomish*
> things spotted from: *Chenies*

solicitors
> excessively elderly: *Skellister*
> fat from Tonbridge Wells:
> > *Valletta*

song
> misheard lyric of: *Rhymney*
> Scottish folk: *Lochranza*
> that makes you want to cry:
> > *Cahors*

sopping, shopping: *Sotterley*

soup
> exotic, made from moats:
> > *Bealings*
> packet: *Poges*
> splattered: *Papple*
> tomato: *Scranton, Tomatin*

space and timelessness: *Hambledon*

spasms, massive facial: *Jawcraig*

speaker
> deliberately ovation-inducing:
> > *Firebag*
> guest, absolute drivel
> > concerning: *Euphrates*

speech
> affected: *Pitroddie*
> fatuous introduction to:
> > *Euphrates*

parts of, crucial, obscured:
> *Dorchester*

sperm
> career-oriented: *Hobarris*
> copious quantities of: *Toronto*
> marooned, damp: *Hobbs Cross*
> marooned, dry: *Bedfont*

spit: *Gallipoli*

spoonful
> eggy: *Symond's Yat*
> not quite a: *Pidney*

spots
> bites which could be: *Bauple*
> to which you have to remain
> > rooted: *Vollenhove*

sprigs, dangling, colorful: *Chenies*

squeezing
> cosmetic: *Quabbs*
> religious: *Clenchwarton*

squiggles, financial: *Albuquerque*

stains
> inky: *Hibbing*
> peanut butter: *Sutton and Cheam*
> trousers, own fault:
> > *Piddletrenthide*
> trousers, not own fault: *Botley*

staircases, winding: *Harbledown*

stairs
> disappearing: *High Limerigg*
> falling down the: *Blean*

standing about: *Lowther*

standing and wondering: *Woking*

standing, ways of: *Ahenny*

stares
> harsh, meaningful: *Kurdistan*
> mellow, meaningless: *Dallow*

state
> disease of deposed heads of:
> > *Patkai Bum*
> hungover: *Duntish*
> of barrister's hair:
> > *Glazeley*
> of dress: *Grinstead*

of mind: *Hynish, Pant-y-Wacco*
of respectable ladies: *Richmond*

steps, small, irrevocable: *Glenties*

stew, ghastly items found in:
Grimsby

stick
out, things that: *Zod, Stebbing,
Huby, Humby, Loberia*
to the point: *Gress*
to your skin, things that:
Wike
together, things that shouldn't
but do: *Dipple*
together, things that won't:
Soller, Badachonacher
up, things that: *Visby, Pymble*

sticks
swiping with: *Hewish*
walking: *Clackmannan*

stomachs
expeditions through seven:
Wendens Ambo
lurching sensations in: *Bedfont*

stories
endless, repetitive, celebrity:
Boothby Graffoe
humorous, heard before:
Plymouth
humorous, interminable:
Gildersome

**strange powers over aircraft
nozzles:** *Ventnor*

stranger, than a zebra: *Yebra*

strangers
perfect, bewildering messages
from: *Berriwillock*
perfect, patronizing remarks
made by: *Maynooth*
perfect, who grab your naughty
bits: *Zagreb*

streaks, brown: *Wyoming*

streets
cleaning of: *Vancouver*
epiglottises spotted on: *Scugog*

exasperating encounters on:
Vollenhove

strips, grimy: *Torlundy*

stubble
in basin: *Hathersage*
in sandwiches: *Munderfield*

stumps, tree: *Baldock*

subject
declaimed ignorantly upon:
Prague
of property prices: *Munster*
someone to unwelcome
attentions: *Boothby Graffoe,
Peterculter, Corfu*

substances
brown, squashy: *Skegness*
green, synthetic: *Halifax*
gray, gummy: *Deal*
ochre, indelicate: *Quabbs*
yellow, dried: *Henstridge*
yellow, squelchy: *Mugeary*
white, flaky: *Skenfrith*
various colors, gushing: *Toronto*

subway
in London: *Amersham, Chicago,
Frant*
in Spring: *Pitsligo*

sunbathing: *Kimmeridge, Kettering*

surprises
hair-induced: *Albacete*
unpleasant, at public school:
Percyhorner

suspicions
horrible: *Mankinholes*
of infidelity: *Kurdistan*

swatting: *Bursledon*

sweat
panther, erotic properties of:
Dunbar
patches of, enticingly displayed:
Pitsligo
patches of, large: *Wedderlairs*
small, moving beads of: *Elsrickle*

swigs, nasty surprises in: *Slumbay*

switches, useless: *Ockle*

T

tables

antique, priceless ruined: *Glossop*

dressing, cluttered with garbage: *Boolteens, Lamlash*

highly polished antique-rosewood dining: *Glossop*

inexpertly laid: *Fentonadle*

leapt onto: *Pabbay*

not setting: *Nanhoron*

shy behavior near: *Namber*

things left on kitchen: *Pudsey*

things stuck under wobbly: *Ludlow*

tactics

diversionary: *Swanage*

thwarted: *Aboyne*

talking, unlikelihood of stopping: *Hove*

taps

pointless: *Pocking*

foot-operated: *Polbathic*

push, trouser-dousing: *Esher*

tarpaulins: *Flodigarry*

taxi drivers: *Fovant*

taxis

driven by idiots: *Lackawanna*

hypocrisy resorted to in: *Crieff*

opinions offered in: *Watendlath*

seductive remarks in: *Low Ardwello*

smell of: *Duluth*

teaspoon, the ultimate: *Scullet*

teeth

feelings in: *Tingrith*

food stores between: *Glutt Lodge*

improvised things used to clean between: *Sigglesthorne*

results of cleaning: *Misool*

things that might have been caused by: *Bauple*

unwelcome views of: *Scugog*

teeth, smiling determinedly through: *Smarden*

telephone directories, collectors of antique: *Aldclune*

telephones

embarrassing memory loss when using: *Gammersgill*

inability to get off: *Harpenden*

numbers, misplaced: *Staplow*

suspicious number of wrong numbers when answering: *Kurdistan*

uselessness of: *Ipswich*

television

afternoons wasted in front of: *Gonnabarn*

celebrity, fat: *Melbury Bubb*

commercials, chuckles at the end of: *Lybster*

interviewers, tone of voice afflicted on: *Scridain*

newscasters, determined not to be embarrassed: *Hosmer*

presenters, tone of voice of: *Tonypandy*

series based on books: *Bathel*

willing to be on: *Sicamous*

theater, practices in: *Hickling, Totteridge, Tabley Superior*

thimbles

conversations that probably touch upon the subject of: *Gussage*

things that aren't: *Pymple*

things

small, complex: *Uttoxeter*

small, pleasant: *Strubby*

small, worrying: *Exeter*

spray, for ironing: *Perranzabuloe*

to do: *Worksop*
various: *Sutton and Cheam*

ties
inelegantly knotted: *Ranfurly*
innate cussedness of:
Clingman's Dome

tights, misuse of: *Grinstead*

tingles
apprehensive: *Ely*
delightful: *Gilling*

tins
attempts to find things to open:
Scosthrop
biscuit: *Lindisfarne*
of emulsion, stubborn: *Botswana*
of soup: *Tomatin*
pyramids of: *Boscastle*

tips, felt: *Scremby*

toasters
spirits that inhabit: *Throckmorton*
uselessness of: *Yate, Burnt Yates*
work, attempts to make:
Throcking

Toblerones, consequences of triangular shape of: *Gubblecote*

toenails, contents of: *Tidpit*

toes, slime on: *Deal*

toiletries
misapplied: *Wollondilly*
mixed: *Glud*
rather naughty: *Spruce Knob*

tongs, silver, for poking Freemasons: *Grimsby*

tongue
things touched with: *Lingle, Moisie*
unwelcome glimpses of: *Scugog*

torches, dim: *Blean*

towels, damp: *Wrabness*

toxic
foreshores: *Spinwam*

soup: *Tomatin*
waste-ground: *Caarnduncan*

tractors, dung-spreading: *Jarrow*

trains
conversations on: *Jawf*
departed without one:
Dunboyne
impersonation of: *Trantlemore, Seattle*
inedible things on: *Amlwch*
non-arrival of: *Amersham*
royal: *Didcot*
tickets: *Nantucket*

trash cans
early warning: *Tananarive*
nasty bits at the bottom of:
Eads
nocturnal behavior of lids of:
Balzan

trees
Nigerian: *Masberry*
stumps of: *Baldock*

tripping over carpet: *Thurnby*

trousers
elderly: *Broats*
inflatable: *Huby*
roguish: *Minchinhampton*
soaking: *Esher*
stained: *Botley, Piddletrenthide*
too long: *Malibu*
wooden: *Goosecruives*
wrong pair of: *Duggleby*

trouts, fierce old: *Baughurst*

trucks, street-cleaning: *Vancouver*

trunks, swimming: *Lubcroy*

truth, palpable: *Hoff*

tubs, impenetrable: *Polloch*

tummies
nasty feelings in pits of: *Ely*
pregnant: *Stowting*
sounds that emanate from:
Tumby

turds
> (dog) comely, well-
> proportioned: *Joliette*
> (dog) small, but still nasty:
> *Bromsgrove*
> thick as your wrist: *Laxobigging*

turn-ups, fertile: *Huttoft*

twats, annoying: *Thrumster*

tweezers, difficulty with: *Hadweenzic*

twerps, bicycle-oriented: *Wormelow Tump*

twitching, uncontrollable: *West Wittering*

of business lunches: *Jeffers*
of dried-up pens: *Kilvaxter*
of epaulettes: *Trossachs*
of keys: *Burton Coggles*
of light switches: *Ockle*
of raincoats: *Plenmeller*
of six ballpoint pens: *Ipplepen*
of telephones: *Ipswich*
of three-color ballpoint pens:
> *Ospringe*
of toasters: *Burnt Yates, Throcking, Throckmorton, Yate*
of trying to attract a bartender's
> attention: *Epping*

usherettes: *Blean*

U

umbrella stands: *Clackmannan*

umbrellas
> absent when needed: *Sotterley, Plenmeller*
> in drinks, stupid little: *Limassol*
> things that aren't: *Dunolly*

underblankets, lumpy: *Tolob*

underclothes, bestrewn: *Adlestrop*

underpant, half an: *Scrabby*

underpants
> floorbound: *Slobozia*
> incomplete: *Scrabby*

undressing
> alarm while watching other
> people: *Wartnaby*
> watching other people: *Beaulieu Hill*

urges, violent: *Kent*

urinals, humiliation at: *Percyhorner*

uselessness
> of acronyms you can never
> remember: *Cafu*
> of bits of the anatomy: *Brecon, Clun*

V

vampire attacks: *Spittal of Glenshee*

vegetables
> abused by Victorians: *Cong*
> colored bits of: *Poffley End*
> display of: *Halifax*

veneer, chipboard: *Mapledurham*

vicars
> entertainment of: *Bude*
> inclinations of: *Lyminster*
> opinions of: *Dean Funes*

virgins, absence of at weddings: *Shirmers*

W

wads, misshapen, squashy: *Pudsey*

waggling, theatrical: *Llanelli*

waiters
> blind: *Epping*
> blue-blooded: *Zlatibor*
> dozy: *Aynho*
> with better memories than you: *Kenilworth*

wallets: *Whasset*

walls

    covered in snitters: *Snitterfield*

    held on by little brass latches:
        Tewel

    inexpertly papered: *Lupridge*

    insufficiently thick: *Boinka*

    kitchen, daubed: *Smearisary*

    people who drive you up:
        Chaling

    run into: *Drumsna*

    satisfying: *Skellow*

wally, a: *Clovis*

wartlike objects: *Kirby Misperton*

washing dishes

    failure to finish properly:
        Abinger, Radlett

    liquid in tea: *Salween*

    nasty bits in: *Scullet, Hadzor*

wasps

    confusion about the color of:
        Wasp Green

    picnics ruined by: *Swaffham
        Bulbeck*

waves

    token: *Sturry*

    unnecessary: *Largoward*

    up trouser: *Malibu*

way up, teeth put back in the
    wrong: *Gipping*

weddings

    friends of bride at: *Shirmers*

    mess caused by: *Pathstruie*

weddings, smoothies at: *Shirmers*

wee

    small hours of the night, things
        that go "ahem" in the:
        Taroom

    small hours of the night, things
        that go bang in the:
        Balzan

    small hours of the night, things
        that gurgle in the: *Bonkle*

wee-wee

    broad jets of: *Spuzzum*

    humorous, artificial: *Barstibley*

    inopportune moment to have
        to have a: *Humby*

    strategies for having a: *Lower
        Peover*

week, day of, deliberate ignorance
    of: *Abligo*

Welsh rarebit, growths on: *Eriboll*

whitebait, pieces of chewed, flying:
    Satterthwaite

willies, insufficiently waggled:
    Piddletrenthide, Botley

Wind, Gone With the: *Epworth*

windbreakers: *Screeb*

wing

    left: *Quedgeley*

    right: *Firebag*

wipers, windshield: *Memphis*

Woolf, Virginia: *York*

words

    deceptive: *Nossob*

    Eskimo: *Anantnag*

    hatefulness of certain:
        Quoyness

    Indonesian, relaxed: *Toodyay*

    people who bang on about:
        Ainderby Quernhow

workman

    cleavage in bottom of:
        Ravenna

    fraudulent: *Podebrady*

wounds

    doubtful: *Hoddlesdon*

    on elbows: *Bures*

wrong

    camera: *Hosmer*

    gone terribly: *Ely*

    place, heart in the: *Willimantic*

    things you're in a mind to get:
        Hynish

Y

yawns
badly supressed: *Wawne*
one who: *Lolland*
things that produce a lot of:
Dolgellau, Rigolet

yearnings
batty: *Abercrave*
nostalgic: *Aberystwyth*

yes
people who won't quite say:
Yetman, Yesnaby

people you would like to say:
Low Ardwello

yes, meaning no: *Yesnaby*

youth
crap about jobs done during:
Pulverbatch
resentment of unfairly
apportioned: *Trunch*

Z

Z, A to: Worgret

Appendix